MEMORIES OF A STAG HARBOURER

Yours Truly
Fred. Goss

(Frontispiece)

MEMORIES OF A STAG HARBOURER

A RECORD OF TWENTY-EIGHT YEARS WITH THE DEVON AND SOMERSET STAG HOUNDS
1894–1921

By

FRED. GOSS

EDITED BY H. CAMPBELL THOMSON, M.D., F.R.C.P.

WITH A PREFACE BY
EARL FORTESCUE

ILLUSTRATED FROM PHOTOGRAPHS

LONDON
H. F. & G. WITHERBY
326 HIGH HOLBORN, W.C.

First published in 1931
Second impression, November 1931
Second facsimile edition published by Halsgrove in 2000

ISBN 1 84114 052 X

British Library Cataloguing in Publication Data
A CIP data record for this book is available from the British Library

HALSGROVE
Publishing, Media and Distribution

Halsgrove House
Lower Moor Way
Tiverton, Devon EX16 6SS
United Kingdom

Tel: 01884 243242
Fax: 01884 243325
www.halsgrove.com

Printed by MPG Books Ltd, Bodmin

PREFACE

No one but its author could have written this little book, for though in France there are many who have a profound knowledge of woodcraft, and though in Scotland there are hundreds of stalkers and others who live among the wild deer and are ever watching them and studying their ways, there is no Englishman like Fred Goss, who has dwelt among them since his birth, and who for three months of every year for twenty-eight years has had to devote from three to six days of every week to the difficult and responsible duties of harbourer.

He was born and brought up in a parish associated for nearly three-quarters of a century with his craft, for old Jim Blackmore who harboured for Mr. Bisset lived at Frogwell Lodge. I never knew him, but Mr. Bisset had great confidence in his skill and capacity. There were very few deer in the county when the pack was revived in 1855 (only eight stags and seven hinds were killed in the first three seasons) so if the stag of the district had for any reason shifted from his usual quarters the day before the meet made for his benefit harbouring became very difficult, and it was common to draw for hours and not uncommon to go several miles, *e.g.* from Sandyway to Badgworthy on 24th August 1857 before beginning.

Old Wensley I knew well; and he deserved all that his grandson says of him and the compliment the stags paid to his funeral; but his activities were limited to the Haddon district.

Miles, who was born and learned his game-keeping in Hampshire, had already been harbourer for a dozen years when I took the hounds, and continued in the post till his death. He was an adept at his work, and loved to follow the chase to its end, for he enjoyed a gallop as much as any man.

I can add little to what Fred Goss tells of his own experiences. His book will, however, be a revelation to hundreds who, even though they may often have hunted with the " Devon and Somerset," have little or no idea of the work that has to be done behind the scenes before the curtain rises on a day's stag hunting, and it should serve to make them less impatient if they have to wait some time before the pack can be laid on.

All lovers of woodcraft will appreciate the keenness of Fred Goss's observation, his interest in animals, his pride in and his devotion to his exacting duties, and the modesty with which he tells his story.

Lord Bayford, for whom he harboured during twelve arduous seasons, once said to me, " Fred's great merit is that he tells you the truth ; if he is not sure of his stag he is not afraid to say so." Such praise of a harbourer is praise indeed.

Fortescue

May 1931.

AUTHOR'S FOREWORD

In the belief that some account of the ways in which a harbourer works and of the insight he gains into the habits of deer will be of interest to followers of the " Devon and Somerset " and others living in the West Country, I have, at the wish of many friends, ventured to record my experiences in this book. My best thanks are due to Dr. Campbell Thomson for the trouble he has taken in editing the reminiscences which I have related to him, and to Mr. Alfred Vowles for so kindly lending me photographs for illustrating the text.

To Earl Fortescue I am especially grateful, both for the Preface and for many helpful suggestions and criticisms given while the book was in the making.

F. G.

2nd IMPRESSION CORRECTION

An error in the first impression, by which the names of Major Adkins and Mr. Stanley were placed in the reverse order to that in which each became Master, has been corrected.

CONTENTS

9

CONTENTS

CONTENTS

LIST OF PLATES

*These illustrations are from photographs kindly provided by the
courtesy of Alfred Vowles of Minehead.*

CHAPTER I   EARLY DAYS

FROM time immemorial Wild Red Deer have lived on Exmoor. Saxon Kings, tradition says, went to Porlock to hunt them. By the Normans they were placed under the forest laws and reserved for royal use. In 1598 the first pack of hounds recorded in the district was kept in the neighbourhood of Simonsbath. From some date between 1724 and 1740 there is, with the exception of two brief periods when hunting was in abeyance (1825–1827 and 1833–1837), a continuous record of successive Masters down to the present day.*

Except for a short season in the spring when three-year-olds are hunted, only stags that have attained the age of five years and upwards are deemed " warrantable " for the chase.

The habits of deer, wandering about the country to feed by night and resting in the depths of woods or amongst interminable tracts of fern on the moor by day, make it impracticable to rely on hounds rousing a warrantable stag in the manner in which fox-hounds set out to find a fox. To try to find a

* See The History of the Forest of Exmoor, by E. T. MacDermot.

suitable deer haphazard at the last moment would be to court failure almost every time. On this account it is necessary for the Master of the Hunt to know whereabouts in the vicinity of the meet a runnable stag " harboureth," *i.e.* the place where he has made his lair. This important piece of information it is the harbourer's business to gather and supply.

The harbourer ranks as one of the regular officials of the Hunt. The qualifications for which he is appointed are general skill in woodcraft combined with special knowledge of deer. His duties are in the main threefold. Firstly he must harbour a " warrantable " deer, secondly he has to report its whereabouts to the Master at the meet ; and thirdly he is called on to assist the huntsman and a few chosen couples of hounds known as the " tufters " to rouse the stag he has previously located. After the stag has been roused and the pack laid on, the huntsman takes charge and the harbourer's work for the day is over. He is then free to go home or join in the hunt as he pleases.

In olden days harbourers used a hound called a " limer " to track deer to their lairs. Limers were so called because they were kept on a " liam " or leash while the deer were being tracked. They were not chosen from any particular breed, their qualifications being a good nose and careful training to follow only certain scents, and never to give tongue while on the line of the quarry.* The limer has long been a thing of the past here, and instead of using a hound harbourers have to depend on their own sight and judgment.

To any one who may be inclined to think harbouring an easy job, I would say : Get up at dawn and make your way to the outskirts of some plantation which deer are known to frequent. There, search the ground around for imprints of their hoofs (" slots "). Having found them, infer from their appearances whether they have been made by a stag or a hind. Should they belong to a stag, what indications do they give of his approximate age and size ? Do the directions the slots take point to the stag having gone into the wood ? If so, does the " freshness " of the slot show the deer has just gone in that morning ? These points being settled to your satisfaction, the question whether the stag has remained in the wood or merely passed through it still remains to be answered. To determine this a tour round the wood must be made and the ground carefully scrutinised to see that no outgoing slots are present.

* The *Manuel de Vénerie Française*, published 1890, devotes a whole chapter to the training and breaking of "limers" which were reckoned to be indispensable to harbourers in France at that date when there were forty packs kept for stag hunting and another sixteen hunted stags in addition to wolves and boars.

Alternatively, take up a position of vantage on the open moor just before daybreak and from there " spot " a herd of stags as they return from their feeding-grounds preparatory to finding resting-places for the day. Scrutinising such a herd carefully through powerful field-glasses, single out a stag that is " warrantable " and watch him to his lair. Then make a mental note of the exact spot with a certainty of being able to lead the huntsman and hounds up to it a few hours later.

Do these things, which in practice are fraught with numberless pitfalls into which the wariest of harbourers may easily walk, and you will have harboured a stag.

To what extent harbourers are born and not made I will not venture an opinion. I can, however, assert freely and without fear of contradiction that inborn aptitude, however great, is of little use without careful training to direct it.

Only by training and experience can any uniformity of success be achieved. Such, indeed, is the complexity of the subject that hunters of olden times recognised no less than seventy-two points regarding the presence of deer and their distinguishing features, though it is confessed that many of these were only modifications of others with new names.

While laying no claim to inborn aptitude I can

certainly congratulate myself on the quality of my teachers, for no man could wish for better than Jim Wensley—my grandfather—and Andrew Miles —the harbourer who preceded me.

I was born at King's Brompton, a little village on the borders of Exmoor and not far from Dulverton. There I lived and went to school until I was fourteen. On leaving school I was sent to Hartford —a hamlet a short distance down the Haddeo Valley in the direction of Dulverton—to live with my grandfather with the idea of following in his footsteps as a carpenter. In addition to his employment of carpenter on the Pixton Estate, of which Hartford forms a part, Jim Wensley, or " Old Jim," as he was familiarly spoken of throughout the countryside, was also by way of being a miller. Remains of the old wooden water-wheel still stand by the side of the mill-house in which Old Jim once lived, and serve as a picturesque reminder of the times when villages needed to be more self-supporting than they do to-day.

Even in my own time, although the railway had already come to the neighbourhood, rough roads and long distances, many of which could only be undertaken on horseback, made getting about difficult to an extent no modern motorist can possibly realise. In winter, villages were not uncommonly isolated for days and even weeks at a stretch, and readers of *Lorna Doone* will recollect from the description of the severe winter at Oare how hard such times could be. Nor is Blackmore's picture of the possibilities of an Exmoor winter unduly exaggerated, for I well recollect a late spring soon after I went to live at Hartford when a trap belonging to Andrew Miles lay embedded in a snowdrift on the road close to Haddon for six weeks. Snow was falling a little in the morning when I drove with him to Bampton in order to take the train to Tiverton, where I accompanied him on some business he had to transact. At Tiverton the weather seemed to improve during the day, but when we started to drive home from Bampton in the evening a regular blizzard had set in. After a detour to avoid a difficult piece of road we had almost reached Haddon when the horse and trap suddenly floundered into a deep drift. With considerable difficulty we succeeded in unharnessing the horse and in making our way home over higher land through the fields. The trap we had to leave to chance. That was the snowstorm in which a man named Cann lost his way on Exmoor and was found dead. Sheep in hundreds were buried in drifts for days before they could be dug out. The swiftly flowing Haddeo and other streams were frozen over, and for weeks afterwards snow was still lying on the ground.

MEMORIES OF A STAG HARBOURER

In those days before gramophones, wireless and such like were ever heard of, villagers had to make their own amusements. Jim Wensley's hobby was natural history, and inspired by him it was not long before I ceased wishing to be a carpenter and turned my attention to becoming a keeper instead.

For any one fond of natural history Hartford was an ideal spot at which to live, and the " King Naturalist," as Jim was once called, made the most of it. His knowledge, which was practical and entirely self-taught from observation, covered a large field relating to all the animals and birds in the district. Foxes, badgers, otters, buzzards and herons all came alike to him, but it was in observing deer that his chief delight lay. For this purpose, the positions of the mill-house and the cottage he built for himself in later years on the hillside just above, were both perfect in commanding a view of Hartford Cleeve on which deer could daily be seen. When crippling rheumatism combined with advancing years prevented him from going far afield, he might still be seen with his telescope tucked under his arm, painfully crawling up to one of his favourite look-out spots. From there, at dawn, he would watch the deer coming over the skyline to enter the woods, and while the morning light was yet too dim for distinguishing details he could tell from the gait and general spread of the antlers what manner of stags they were. Among followers of the " Devon and Somerset " Old Jim could claim friends innumerable, to whom in his inimitable " Zummerzet " he has given many a useful " tip " as to the direction a stag that was being hunted around Haddon would be likely to take. Jim Wensley was born in 1831 and died in 1912. As his funeral left the cottage door a herd of nineteen *girt* big stags stood looking down from the top of Haddon to watch the old man's passing— a compliment which, could he have known, he would above all things have appreciated.

Jim Wensley was at no time official harbourer to the " Devon and Somerset," as sometimes erroneously stated, but he often harboured locally when meets were held on the Pixton Estate. He also gave Andrew Miles, who at that time harbourer to the Hunt and keeper for the Haddon district, a good deal of friendly assistance, especially in Miles' latter years when his health was failing. Luckily for me, whenever Jim went on his harbouring expeditions he liked to take me with him, and under his able tuition I soon learnt to sum up the characters of a " warrantable " deer.

In " slotting," Old Jim had acquired extraordinary skill, and the instructions he imparted to me for estimating the sex, age, approximate size and weight of deer by this method laid a sure foundation of knowledge on which I could build later. At eighteen there occurred the opportunity of my becoming under-keeper to Miles. This suited me admirably, for on discovering I possessed sufficient knowledge about deer to be useful, Miles began to ask me to help him with the harbouring. Assisting at Haddon meets led to going further afield, a treat I always looked forward to and thoroughly enjoyed.

Then the great day came when I was given an opportunity of showing what I could do on my own. The meet was to be at Haddon, and as Miles was not feeling well he asked me to take a look round the lower woods while he explored the upper ones. Thereupon I set off for Storridge Wood, one of the largest of the Haddon woods, and one in which deer can nearly always be found. A little way outside the plantation lying just above the wood I came upon freshly made slots leading into the wood. These clearly belonged to a large stag. After a careful search all round the wood without finding anything to indicate that the deer had left, I hurried back with my information to Hartford. There fortune further favoured me, for Miles, who was waiting to hear my report, had not that morning happened to have harboured a stag of any size, and was in consequence all the more ready to listen to me. After hearing what I had to say he rode off to inspect the slots for himself, and being satisfied they were those of a runnable stag he without more ado accepted my word for it that the stag was still in the wood. This I took as a great compliment, since the outlook for the day's sport depended largely on my being right. A few hours later I had the satisfaction of seeing my conclusions verified when Anthony Huxtable took the tufters into the wood and roused a big old stag with only one horn. A good run of some twenty miles took the hounds to Hurlstone Point near Porlock, where the stag succeeded in cleverly evading the pursuers and escaped. For the Field the run had been enjoyable, and for me—I had harboured my first stag! Three weeks or so later this same old stag, having in the meantime returned to his old haunts, as deer so often will, was again roused in Haddon, this time from Hurscombe Wood. Doubtless recollecting the happy termination of the previous run, he took the hounds over almost exactly the same line of country and again finished up at Hurlstone Point. On this occasion, however, the end was less fortunate for him.

Increasing ill-health caused Miles to lean more and more on me for assistance, and before his death took place I had gained a very considerable amount of first-hand experience. He died in

MEMORIES OF A STAG HARBOURER

April 1894, leaving the posts of keeper at Haddon and harbourer to the Hunt both vacant.

The appointment of keeper lay in the hands of the Pixton Estate, and carried with it the cottage known as Frogwell Lodge on the top of Haddon. Though this was known as the " Harbourer's Cottage " on account of Miles and, before him, Jim Blackmore having lived there, it belonged to the Pixton Estate and was not the property of the Hunt. Wishing to get married and not thinking my chances of becoming harbourer were too great, I turned my attention especially towards obtaining the post of keeper, so that I might secure the cottage to live in. To this end I made personal application to Mr. Stevens, the estate agent.

" You will be the keeper, whatever the Hunt may decide about the harbourer," was in effect his reassuring reply, to which, with a joke about " possession being nine points of the law," he added that the keys of the cottage would be given to me as soon as Mrs. Miles was prepared to leave.

This initial success put me in good heart to apply for the post of harbourer, though for that I feared my youth would tell against me. After talking things over with Jim Wensley I decided to make my ambition known to Mr. Basset, a former Master of the " Devon and Somerset," who knew something of my work. The warm letter of encouragement I received from Mr. Basset on the top of a favourable interview kindly granted me by Mr. Philip Everard, at that time Hon. Secretary of the Hunt, gave me good reason to hope for success, and out of a number of applicants the choice of the Master—Colonel Hornby—and the Hunt Committee eventually fell on me.

Thereupon in May 1894, when I had just turned twenty-one, I commenced my duties, in the course of which I was destined to serve for twenty-eight years under seven successive Masters, and to harbour upwards of twelve hundred stags.

CHAPTER II   HARBOURING IN GENERAL

ON taking up my duties as keeper and harbourer I moved into the cottage known as Frogwell Lodge on the top of Haddon Hill, where Jim Blackmore and Andrew Miles had lived before me. It thus maintained its right to the popular title of the " Harbourer's Cottage," and retained it for a further ten years until on becoming head keeper to the Pixton Estate my work took me to live at Weir.

At the time of my appointment the system known as local harbouring was to some extent still in vogue. It consisted in keepers and others who claimed to possess special knowledge of the habits of deer being asked to harbour for meets held on their respective employers' estates. The assumption was that their daily routine work gave them a good inkling of the probable whereabouts of a stag, for the finding of which they also received a perquisite in the shape of the harbouring fee. In practice this scheme had not been working satisfactorily, partly on account of the divided responsibility, and also on account of the frequency with which the amateurs failed to harbour a warrantable stag. The custom was therefore allowed to die out, and within two years or thereabouts of taking up the work I found myself responsible for harbouring over practically the whole of the Devon and Somerset country. This comprises a large area extending roughly from Barnstaple at the one end to the Quantocks on the other, and includes within its boundaries the whole of Exmoor. This necessarily often entailed long journeys to distant meets, all of which in those pre-motor days had to be made on horseback. At the end of my first season Colonel Hornby resigned and was succeeded by Mr. R. A. Sanders, now Lord Bayford, the title by which I shall in future refer to him. The deer about that period had multiplied so greatly that it became a problem to keep them within reasonable limits. How numerous they were may be gathered from the fact that one day when hounds were out and deer were on the move, I counted no less than seventy-two in one herd. They were jumping a fence in single file, just like sheep following one another, and were making their way from Winsford Hill down into the Barle Valley.

After some consideration it was decided to hunt more often, and meets were arranged for Monday, Wednesday, Thursday and Saturday of each week, the Master hunting hounds himself one day a week in order to give his huntsman—who on that day acted as Whip—a rest. This meant that no sooner had I seen one stag away than I often had to be off as quickly as I could, perhaps some fifteen miles or so across country, in order to harbour another stag for the following day.

If things got too busy I could always rely on getting help from Jim Wensley for the Haddon meets so long as he remained active enough to get about. The old man was a great stickler for punctuality, and with the habit some grandfathers have in refusing to recognise that their grandsons have grown up, he never hesitated to give me a " piece of his mind " whenever occasion seemed to him to require it.

By good luck more than good management I contrived one morning not only to escape a wigging, but to score off the old man as well. The occasion was a meet at Haddon, for which we had arranged to be at Hartford together at 6 a.m. to harbour a stag. That morning I unfortunately overslept myself—a most unusual occurrence—and woke to hear the clock striking the appointed hour. After dressing hurriedly I saddled my horse and set off by a short cut over the heather instead of taking the longer way by the road. I had not ridden down the hill very far when suddenly the tops of a pair of antlers came into view above the banks of a deep gully, up which a stag was evidently coming. Instantly slipping out of the saddle I concealed myself in the heather in such a way that I could look under the horse's belly and see what was happening.

Slowly the horns continued to move along the gully until finally the stag came into view. On reaching the open he stopped and gazed suspiciously in my direction, but as the wind was blowing from him toward me and he saw nothing but the horse his suspicions were allayed, and quite unconcerned he turned away and sauntered off towards Hartford Cleeve.

After giving the deer time to get well out of sight I rode on down the hill to find Jim, fuming with rage, waiting for me at the bottom.

" Thought 'ee was going to be here at zix o'clock," he shouted angrily as I came within earshot.

" Haven't you seen anything on the Cleeve ? " I retorted in a tone that carried a faint suggestion of surprise that he had missed something. " Because a big stag I've been watching has just come in there."

This took the wind out of the old man's sails, and without further argument about the time he hurried to his cottage for the telescope. On scanning the side of the hill we soon spotted the stag in the act of beating a withy bush preparatory to settling down for a comfortable rest, only to be rudely disturbed a little later on when the tufters came to look for him. A good run followed which ended in a kill at Coomberow under the Brendon Hills.

In the ordinary routine of harbouring my custom was to arrive at the neighbourhood in which I wanted to locate a stag some time during the afternoon of the day immediately preceding the meet. This gave me time to find whereabouts the stags were so that I could finally confirm their presence in some particular wood the next morning. A preliminary look round some of the coverts which deer were likely to be frequenting often resulted in useful information being obtained from " racks." These are the gaps deer make in the fences in travelling to and fro between the woods and the feeding-grounds, and are easily discernible while riding on horseback. If on examining the racks and feeding-grounds slots are seen, the question as to whether there are warrantable deer about is often soon settled. Discovery of slots in this way makes an excellent beginning, especially if the harbourer is in a part of the country with which he happens not to be very familiar. For deer are very faddy in their choice of places for resting, and without local knowledge it is possible to waste a lot of time in looking round woods which they perhaps seldom enter. There are some woods which it is rare for anything but hinds to frequent ;

others are preferred only by stags. Some, again, are cared for by neither hinds nor stags, though why this should be so I do not know. Having discerned slots in the racks or on the feeding-grounds, it is a good plan to erase some of them with the point of a stick, so that fresh ones can be detected without any trouble the next morning when the presence of the stag has finally to be confirmed. Care must, however, be taken not to interfere in any way with the rack itself, for in summer-time when food is plentiful and easily come by, deer are very suspicious, and any disturbance of the fence where they pass through, such as the dislodgment of a stick or two, will often put them off. In winter when food is scarce they become bolder and less particular.

Putting together all the available evidence as I went along, my next step was to supplement it by hearing what the farmers in the district had to say, and for their assistance and for the open-handed hospitality I received from them I shall always be grateful. Many are the occasions when I have thus been put on the lines for making a successful harbour which vagaries of weather—to the influence of which I shall allude later—and other unexpected circumstances would otherwise have made difficult to bring off.

When no news of deer was available, it might be

necessary to look round half a dozen or more coverts of anything from a few hundred yards to four miles or so in length, before coming upon tracks that were of any use. Moreover, I liked, if possible, always to have two strings to my bow, for stags have an uncanny way of divining when something unusual is in the air, and here to-night and gone to-morrow is a possibility that always has to be reckoned with. For weeks on end they will frequent a wood regularly, and then for no apparent reason they will suddenly shift their quarters on the very morning on which one is relying on them being there.

As soon as I felt I had conclusive evidence of a warrantable stag—or two if possible—being near at hand, I felt justified in knocking off work for the day and going to the farm-house at which hospitality was being offered me for the night. And very lucky in this respect I consider myself to have been, for I had homes of refuge in every district. So frequent were my harbouring visits to some parts that a room was not unfrequently called " mine " for the season. A brief chat and then early to bed was the programme, for I had to be up again before dawn in order to see the stags coming in on the forest or if possible to catch a view of one going into the woods. It was in these early hours that final evidence of the precise

c

whereabouts of a warrantable stag had to be obtained either by seeing the deer or by such other signs as I felt able conclusively to accept. Seeing the deer is obviously the most satisfactory way of judging its qualities. With care this can often be managed from a rising knoll, a mere glimpse of the animal or even of its antlers being to the practised eye all that is usually necessary for the purpose. But however carefully the observation posts may be chosen both for concealment and for the way of the wind, the stag may still become suspicious and all at once decide to put several miles of country between himself and the origin of his fears.

The possibility of this untoward event happening obliges the harbourer to stay on the watch for perhaps another hour or two, and finally to ride or walk round all that part of the wood hitherto hidden from view in order to be sure by the absence of slots that the stag has not gone out of the wood on the other side. In many parts of the enclosed country it is not possible to find a suitable spot from which anything of a view can be obtained, and in such circumstances the harbourer has to fall back on other signs among which slotting takes first place. By this method, as described in detail in the following chapter, a stag that has not been seen can, nevertheless, be estimated as warrantable or otherwise and tracked with certainty to its lair.

On the open moor, where there are no woods into which deer can be slotted, the harbourer relies almost entirely on sight. Here, as in the wooded country, deer show definite likes and dislikes to certain districts. To this extent the harbourer knows by experience whereabouts deer are most likely to be found, but even then the tracts of moor are so extensive as to make harbouring a lengthy and often a very tricky business. On the other hand, stags are easier to see on the moor than among the woods, but the choice of a suitable spot for viewing them has, nevertheless, to be very carefully made both as regards the way of the wind and the locality of the feeding-grounds from which the deer may be expected to return. To view stags in these circumstances it is essential to be on the moor before daybreak, which is the time they always choose to come in from their feeding-grounds to rest. The etiquette observed by stags on these occasions is most entertaining. With an old and experienced "Master stag" leading, the rest of the herd follow in single file. Every few hundred yards or so the leader stops to look round and sniff the air for signs of danger, and simultaneously the other members of the column stop also. Not on any account must one of the lesser lights ever get in front. If, after due investigation of the surroundings, the leader is satisfied that all is well, off they all start again and continue until the next check, when the same performance is repeated. Finally, on arriving at a place which looks inviting, the leader halts the column, and turning round to face his faithful followers, he makes them what looks for all the world like a polite bow. This signifies their dismissal, and the great personage thereupon proceeds to walk off haughtily into the fern to find himself a comfortable place on which to lie. Having found a spot to his liking, he turns round a few times like a dog making his bed and leisurely settles down. On their dismissal his retinue likewise disperse to their beds. In doing so they must not lie down near enough to encroach on their leader's privacy. Nor, on the other hand, must they go too far away, for old stags, whether on the moor or in the woods, always like to have younger ones close at hand for drawing off hounds or bearing the brunt of other dangers which their elders feel disinclined to face. I believe it is sometimes stated that on approaching their resting-places stags will leap over the last few yards of ground with the idea of breaking the continuity of scent between their tracks and their lair. I have seen them act in this way when hard pressed by hounds, though whether it was with the object of breaking the line of scent I cannot say ; but when going to their resting-places in the ordinary way I have never seen them do other than walk up to the spot, turn round a few times and lie down. As soon as deer can be seen on the skyline the harbourer singles out a runnable stag and keeps it in sight until it settles down. To do this efficiently requires powerful field-glasses, two pairs of which I am fortunate to possess. The first pair was presented to me a long time ago by many followers of the Hunt, and the second pair was a gift from the late Mr. Badco during the time he was Master. Before then I used to use an old-fashioned pair which necessitated a much closer approach to the stags to enable me to judge their points, and the new ones were also a tremendous advantage when looking for deer after they had settled down amongst the bracken. Even with the aid of good glasses the task is by no means easy, for stags vary in appearance so much according to the light and surroundings that nothing short of long experience enables one to say which is " warrantable " and which is not.

Mr. Philip Everard rightly emphasises this difficulty when he says that the art of judging what stags are big enough or warrantable, as they are viewed under the different conditions and surroundings during the hunting season, is one of the last attainments of a finished stag-hunter ; so different does the same deer appear according to the various lights and shades, the direction and pace the animal is travelling ; whether it is coming towards or away from the observer, or viewed from a height or on a level plain, that when seen on one occasion it may look to be quite a different size as compared with its appearance another time.*

Whilst not neglecting to notice the gait and general bulk of body, both of which afford indications of importance, it is on the antlers the harbourer chiefly fixes his attention. The manner of their " spread " and the number of " points " they bear, give him the principal information he requires, the details and conclusions to be drawn from which are described later.

Once the stag has thoroughly settled down in a comfortable bed of fern he usually remains there unless accidentally disturbed by a stray sheep-dog or some unusual noise or smell that makes him afraid. The longer he has settled down the closer in the face of danger he will be likely to lie, a fact that comes out strongly when "tufting." It is while they are on the move early in the morning that deer are so apt to take to flight, and if once they are thoroughly startled they may go for miles before they stop.

* *Stag-hunting with the Devon and Somerset, 1887-1901.*

CHAPTER III SLOTS AND SLOTTING

FAILING a view of the stag which in wooded districts, as the reader will have already gathered, is by no means always easy to obtain, the harbourer turns his attention to other signs. Among these are imprints of hoofs ("slots"), droppings ("fumes" or " fewmets "), and evidence of recent feeding in turnip fields, cornfields, orchards and elsewhere. To see shoots of a young ash that have recently been picked off is also a sure sign of deer being about, and many a good stag have I harboured that has been no further afield to feed than the ash fence round the covert in which he was lying hidden.

To be able to see a stag is often very convenient, especially when woods adjoin heather-covered ground on which slotting is impossible. A view is, however, by no means essential, for given suitable conditions nothing gives more satisfactory results than slotting. I know few things more fascinating than to find where a big stag has been feeding, to slot him into the wood, and afterwards to cast all round the wood along fences, lanes and roads, to see if he has walked out again. Slotting

39

a stag in this way from feeding-ground to resting-place, and making sure by casting round that he has not moved, gives the harbourer a confidence in making his report to the Master that not even a view of the stag at close quarters could strengthen.

Slotting is a many-sided art. It entails accurate observation from which the truth of the inferences to be drawn are quickly tested by the hounds. Variations in soil and weather as well as peculiarities in the deer themselves all combine to add to the interest.

Slot is the term by which the feet of deer are known, and also of the imprint their feet make in the ground. Slots are prized trophies of the chase. They are presented by the Master, after the kill, to the lucky few, among whom youngsters in at the death of their first stag often find themselves favourably regarded.

A deer's foot is built for strength and elasticity. Strong, swiftly to carry the heavy head and body away from danger, it has to be; nor is the necessity for elasticity to withstand the shocks from constant jumping any less.

The division of the foot into two parts—the cloven hoof—also serves a useful purpose, for " it prevents the foot sinking into soft ground and permits it to be more easily withdrawn."* Compared with a horse's foot, which in its concave form,

* *The Hand,* by Sir Charles Bell.

says this same authority, " is attended with a vacuum or suction as it is withdrawn . . . the split and conical shaped hoof (of the deer) expands in sinking and is easily extricated." The ability possessed by deer for travelling over soft ground where horses are unable to follow is of great advantage to them, and I have never seen deer become bogged as sometimes happens to horses.

The necessity, when slotting, for paying close attention to the nature of the soil has already been mentioned, for the soil is a factor that must always be taken into consideration when deductions are being made. In peaty soil such as abounds on many parts of the forest, the edges of the imprints tend to contract somewhat after the animal has passed, thereby giving an impression that the deer is smaller than it actually is. A similar tendency to contraction of the slot also occurs in sand of certain consistency, such as frequently exists in the beds of partially dried-up water-courses.

Clay soil and heavy plough land on the contrary tend, on account of their soft and slippery surfaces, to make the slots larger than they should be, and so give an erroneous idea of a bigger stag.

On firm soil and dusty surfaces of hard roads the slots correspond exactly in size with the hoofs that make them, and no allowances when estimating them need be made.

MEMORIES OF A STAG HARBOURER

The first essential in slotting is to learn to distinguish the slot of a stag from that of a hind. Up to the age of two the differences are slight and differentiation difficult, though even at that age an expert can frequently detect the slightly broader toes that indicate the male. From two upwards the differences become increasingly clear. The toes of a hind are long and narrow. Their slots are smaller, shallower, more pointed and, on account of lighter weight, less sharply defined and altogether more " lady-like " than those of stags which have broad square toes and large and weighty heel marks. The front slots of a good huntable stag, which are those by which I always judge, should be square, with the toes well blunted and worn back from constantly alighting on them in jumping. Here, again, the consistency of soil and general nature of the country to which the stag has been accustomed must be taken into account, for where ground is soft and fences few, as for example on parts of the forest, the effects of jumping will be less pronounced than in country of opposite character. A Haddon deer, for instance, will, other things being equal, show a slightly different shaped slot from that of a deer of corresponding size on the forest. The weight of a heavy stag coming on the ground also opens out the heel to an extent not seen in young stags. Thus the slot of a big heavy stag should be practically square. Each claw of a good warrantable stag should be at least an inch wide, but the measurement of the slot as a whole will, as previously indicated, depend to some extent on the soil in which it is planted.

I also like to see the toes of a slot turn a little outwards. Elderly stags, like elderly men, walk somewhat differently from young ones, and a slot with toes turned outwards always indicates age.

On soft ground, stags, especially while galloping, often leave a big impression of their dew claws. These make a formidable show, and are to some degree indicators of size. It is, however, the pace the animal is travelling rather than its weight that determines the impact, so that I have never regarded them as of any special significance. Indeed, I would rather find slots without them, for as indicators of pace they suggest the stag has been disturbed.

On very hard or stony ground on which an impression is not easily made, it occasionally happens that only the bare outline of a hoof can be detected. It has somewhat the appearance of an outline made by a lead pencil on the faces of stones in a field or on the hard surface of a road. It is due to the margins of the horny substance growing faster than the inner parts of the

43

hoof, and thus making only an outline on the hard surface on which it alights, without leaving any other details. It signifies weight, and to me it has always been known as a shell slot, which was the name handed down by Jim Wensley who first acquainted me with its importance in indicating the presence of a big stag. I have never seen this variety of slot made by young deer.

The relative positions occupied by fore and hind slots are of importance when stags are walking. In young stags they practically coincide, that is, the hinder slot falls into the fore slot so that it almost covers it. In older stags the hinder slot falls slightly more behind. In stags the front slot is rather larger than the back one, while in hinds they are both about the same size. Deviations from the relative positions of front and back slots are dealt with at some length in *Forest Creatures*,* and are said to signify corresponding changes in the movements and positions of the hind quarters. For instance, the slot of a stag's hind leg that falls slightly on the outer side of the one made by the fore leg indicates his hind quarters are bulging outwards with venison and indicates size. If in addition to falling slightly to the outer side the hinder slot also lags a little behind the fore one,

* *Forest Creatures*, by Charles Boner, describing the habits of stags and other wild animals in the forests of Germany.

44

the indication is that of a particularly large stag. In my own experience I have generally found that any departure from the normal relative positions of fore and hinder slots denotes size, since the cause of the change in position is nearly always due to the inability of a fat stag to move the slot as far forward as one in poorer condition.

Slots vary in appearance according to the pace a deer is travelling. In galloping, the slots are naturally much further apart than when walking, and on soft ground the hoofs sink deeper than when walking. Speed also induces the toes to spread, and so gives rise to a broader moulding of the soil between the claws. The broader the moulding is between the claws, the heavier the animal may be considered to be. In judging the pace which deer have passed along hard roads the same principles are applicable, but the hoofs do not, of course, sink in as they do in softer soil. When being hunted, deer will sometimes run for quite a distance along roads. The huntsman and whips often then have to do some slotting to see which way the deer has gone, for roads are bad for scent and hounds find difficulty in hunting on them. Directly the deer leaves the hard road hounds pick up the line without difficulty and are off again.

A good sign of an old stag, whether the slots are

large or not, is a difference in the length of the two claws of one foot, one claw being sometimes a good deal longer than the other. This inequality, for some reason I cannot explain, most frequently occurs in the left hinder slot, though I have

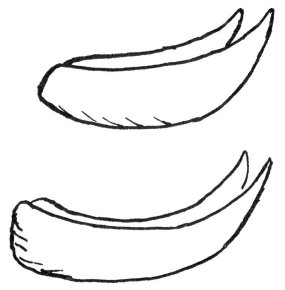

SKETCH FROM MEMORY OF DEFORMED SLOTS

occasionally seen it in the fore slot. Even though the slots may be smaller than one would expect I have never, when this difference in length has been present, known them to belong to anything but an old stag.

Many slight variations in the appearance of slots which to the practised eye often mean a great deal, are almost impossible to put into words, and to be properly appreciated they must be seen. A slot made in the morning, for instance, differs from one made the night before by a certain freshness about it that is not easy to describe. A stag passing from grass on to a road in the dewy morning will carry a certain amount of moisture with the slot, while one going off the road on to a field will carry with it traces of dust.

Malformed slots are sometimes met with. I remember as a boy, when Earl Fortescue was Master, a stag being killed at Haddon with all four feet deformed. I am indebted to Earl Fortescue for the accompanying sketch from memory of the appearance of two of these slots. This stag, Earl Fortescue states, appeared to be five or six years old, and though the peculiarity of the slots was well known to Andrew Miles, the harbourer at that time, the stag had never been found by the hounds until the day on which he was killed.

Another stag—a three-year-old with somewhat similar deformities—I remember being found in Haddon and killed at Hele Bridge when Mr. Stanley was Master. As far as I recollect only two feet were deformed in this instance. The toes were very long and turned up somewhat like those of the stag mentioned by Earl Fortescue, but in this last case the toes of both deformed feet were overriding each other. I have seen peculiarities of this

47

kind more often in fallow deer than wild deer, such deformities being decidedly rare among the latter.

When slots are disproportionally small the harbourer is naturally apt to discard them for something more substantial, and this probably accounts for a certain number of old stags being overlooked until they are actually seen. One old stag, a slot of which I still possess, well illustrates this point. I first heard of him when I was one day harbouring for a meet on Molland Common. A farmer in the district assured me a *girt* big stag was in the habit of feeding regularly on the farm and had recently been seen in a plantation of young firs.

On riding round the fields there were plenty of slots to be seen where the deer had been feeding, but nothing to indicate anything greater than a four-year-old. That being of no use to me I went further afield and harboured a stag elsewhere. Not very long afterwards I found myself harbouring in the same district again, and again the same farmer repeated the story of a stag with a " terrible big head " having been recently seen. Another careful search revealed nothing more than the slots of a four-year-old, and again I went on to harbour elsewhere. This time, however, the farmer sent a boy after me in the evening to say the stag was out feeding and could be seen if I cared to come back. Having harboured nothing else in the meantime, it seemed worth while to return. On being told of the stag's whereabouts I soon caught sight of him and knew at once the farmer had been quite right. On a body of comparatively small size, which accounted for the undersized slots, was set an enormous head carrying no less than seventeen points.

On going round the fields early the next morning to make sure the stag of the night before was still there, I found evidence showing that another stag had come in from the common during the night and had also gone into the same wood. From the slots alone the new one would have been judged the better stag, but having seen the other I knew, of course, the new one would not have such a good head. As luck would have it, when the tufters came to draw they put up the last arrival first, and as the general rule is to follow the first good stag that goes away rather than risk loss of time and possible disappointment in looking longer for a particular one, the older inhabitant was left undisturbed.

His time, however, came later on in the same season when I was harbouring for a meet at Hawkridge. From a position I had taken up close to Brewers Castle—a well-wooded earthwork of ancient origin on the banks of the Barle—I could hear a stag roaring in a way that made me think he was accompanied by hinds. From the varying directions in which the belling came I judged the deer were on the move, and having an idea they would very likely cross the river and go into Mouncey Castle*—a wooded hill of similar nature on the opposite bank—I carefully concealed myself and waited. What I surmised might happen soon came to pass, and the stag accompanied by a single hind came out of the wood and crossed the river as I had anticipated. No sooner did I cast eyes on him than I recognised my old friend of the seventeen points, and as soon as he had gone well out of sight I looked carefully at his slots again. There was no doubt about their exceptionally small size, and indeed it would have puzzled anyone who had not seen the two deer pass to say which was the slot of the stag and which of the hind. When the tufters went into Mouncey Castle they roused him almost immediately, and I still have a vivid recollection of the " view-halloa " given by that accomplished and veteran stag-hunter, Mr. Froude Hancock, when he saw the big-headed deer breaking covert. Nor was the subsequent run to be despised. Away to Exford, back along again over Winsford Hill and thence across South Hill, where came a check through

* Also spelt Mounsey and Mountsey.

Sidney Tucker's horse falling and knocking the wind out of its rider. Lord Bayford at once had the hounds stopped, but timely aid from Dr. R. J. Collyns soon put Sidney back into the saddle. The hounds were then laid on again, and in spite of the delay they soon came up with the stag not far from the spot from which we had started in the morning.

The peculiarities in the slots of this stag interested me so much that I asked the Master to give me one as a memento of the occasion. This request was kindly granted, and I still have the slot which I value not only for the memories it brings back, but also because it is the only slot I ever had given to me in my life. I have often shown it to my friends as the slot of the deer that for so long managed to deceive me. The head of this stag was a particularly fine one, and I have harboured only one other carrying the same number of points. That also was during the time Lord Bayford was Master, and in my opinion it was the record head of that period.

Seventeen points is a large number for West Country deer to carry. The only one I have heard of with more is the famous Badgworthy deer with nineteen points, chronicled by Dr. Palk Collyns* as having been killed in 1786.

* *Chase of the Wild Red Deer.*

THE final duties of the harbourer consist in being present at the meet to report to the Master where a warrantable stag can be found, and in afterwards assisting the huntsman and tufters to rouse him. Until then a wise harbourer keeps his knowledge to himself lest curiosity on the part of onlookers should lead to the stag being disturbed. The report, which the Field eagerly awaits, since on it largely depends their chance of a day's sport, is followed by a brief consultation between the Master, harbourer and huntsman concerning the best tactics to pursue. Four or five couples of the older and more trusty hounds are then selected for tufting, the remainder of the pack being kennelled at some neighbouring farm or other building conveniently near by until they are wanted for the "lay on." Those who are unfamiliar with the methods of stag-hunting do not always understand the necessity for tufting which is required on account of the large size of the woods and the numbers of deer inhabiting them. To use the whole pack for rousing a deer under such conditions would inevitably result in the hounds breaking up into small groups and hunting all and sundry deer they happened to find, while the oldest stags would, with their well-known cunning, take advantage of the confusion by making sure that hounds should follow any other trail but theirs. It does sometimes happen when a stag has been harboured on the open moor that the pack can be used straight away to rouse him. The circumstances in which this is advisable are, however, exceptional, and tufting, tedious to onlookers as it doubtless sometimes is, has to be the general rule.

The hounds selected for tufting are chosen for their general sagacity and willingness to work. They must have good noses and on entering a covert, they should " draw away " at the huntsman's bidding and hunt the thicket on their own, coming together again at the first challenge of any one of them to assist in taking up the line. They must also give tongue well so that the huntsman can tell what they are doing when he is unable to see them. In giving tongue hounds vary greatly. Some speak so clearly that an experienced huntsman will go so far as to say he can tell whether they are hunting a stag or a hind. Others run almost mute. Above all things, tufters must be obedient, for not only are they required to stop on the word of command when following unwarrantable stags or hinds, but they must also be stopped after they have run their warrantable stag sufficiently far into the open country for the pack to be laid on. Good tufters can be stopped without difficulty, and a pretty sight it is to see them give up their hunting and sit down to wait patiently for the pack as knowingly as we do ourselves.

The best tufter I ever knew, and I have met with a great many in my time, was a black-and-white hound called Worcester, during the time Lord Bayford was Master. No matter how dense the wood or how scentless the day, it had to be a very clever stag that escaped Worcester's attentions. A " hold-hard-old-man " always brought him to a standstill immediately, and for general sagacity I doubt whether Whyte-Melville's *Tancred* and *Tarquin* of Katerfelto fame could have beaten him. One day I remember when we were drawing Whitechapel Wood near South Molton, all the tufters except Worcester came out of the wood without finding anything. On Sidney Tucker observing Worcester was not with them I proposed we should wait a few minutes to see what the hound was doing. Sure enough we soon heard Worcester giving tongue from the far end of the wood. The other tufters were at once sent back to help him,

54

TYPICAL TUFTERS

and after a brief interval they roused one of the most beautiful stags I have ever seen break covert. There were many other occasions when Worcester distinguished himself in a similar fashion. On one of them his daring or impudence, as no doubt the stag regarded it, nearly led to his undoing. I had harboured a stag in Thorney Cleeve Wood for a Yard Down meet, and, incidentally, this was the first time I had known deer to be lying on the west side of the Bray Valley.

Worcester, as usual, was the first to be picked of the four couples chosen for tufting, and such was the confidence we put in him to find the stag that the huntsman and I did not trouble to go into the wood ourselves, but were content to ride along the road below it. After a little time we heard Worcester baying all right and then suddenly the note changed into a long-drawn-out howl. This at once brought the other tufters to his side, and shortly after that a big stag broke covert and came in our direction with the tufters close at his heels.

After the tufters had been stopped and while the pack was being brought along, we examined Worcester and found he had been rather badly gored. With help from the huntsman's " first-aid " case the wound was stitched up and the hound sent back to Exford. A good recovery resulted and old Worcester lived to take part in many a good hunt after that. The stag that gored him was an old one with only one horn. After giving hounds a fairly good run he was eventually accounted for in a meadow on Nadrid Farm. This was the biggest stag I have ever seen killed. Without the head and after the carcase had been " dressed," it weighed 16 score and 4 lb., or 23 stone 1 lb. without head, skin or slots. The head of this stag now adorns the walls of Gratton Farm near High Bray.

The procedure of tufting is carried out by the huntsman, harbourer and tufters entering the wood with the express object of rousing the particular deer that has previously been harboured. Unless some other deer equally worthy of attention breaks covert first, they continue their search until they either find the stag or are forced to conclude he is no longer there.

The direction in which the covert is drawn is the one that seems most likely to drive the stag into open country with the object of ensuring a good run. While tufting is proceeding inside the wood, the whips and a few of the more experienced members of the Hunt are posted at suitable points outside to watch what comes out. Among these Mr. Froude Hancock was always numbered, and no better sportsman or better judge of a stag ever rode after a pack of hounds.

MEMORIES OF A STAG HARBOURER

To find a stag in the midst of acres of dense undergrowth is not such an easy task as some might think. Those who sometimes find the delay tedious should try to picture the huntsman and harbourer coaxing their mounts through unending entanglements of fern and briar on a grilling day in August when, maybe, there is no scent to help. Under such conditions stags have only to lie close enough and they will often escape detection. It is indeed surprising how close they will lie, for, unlike a fox that pricks up its ears at the first unusual sound and slinks away, once stags have thoroughly settled down for the day they are very loth to shift again. In the early morning when they are on the move the slightest suspicion of danger may, as already noted, set them off galloping for miles, but once they have settled in to rest their first line of defence lies in their efforts to remain unseen. The general disturbance in the neighbourhood inseparable from a meet and the sound of the horn as hounds approach the covert serve to make them lie all the closer. Squatting in the depths of a dense bed of fern with noses on the ground and antlers laid back almost parallel with their bodies, stags will lie so securely concealed that short of stumbling on them accidentally, they remain almost undiscoverable. To the practised eye it is the sight of their antlers that not infrequently reveals their presence. They have considerable difficulty in hiding these, and it needs only the tip of one projecting through the fern to give the animal away, while its owner, all unconscious of having been seen, clings closer to the ground than ever. Without some luck of this sort, days that are scentless for hounds are full of hard work and frequent disappointment for the harbourer, for the intense heat and oppressive air in a bed of high ferns are very trying and often make it very difficult for hounds to wind a deer. While the wood is being drawn hopes raised by the sounds of deer breaking away are time after time frustrated by finding the quarry roused are only hinds or young male deer. Back come the tufters to begin the search again, and only when to the accompaniment of loud shouts and crashing undergrowth the " view-halloa " proclaims the wanted stag has at last broken covert, can the harbourer rest content that his work is done.

One day early in my career it was only by the merest chance that a disappointment of this kind was averted. The weather was very hot and a large field was impatient to be off when neither of two stags I had confidently harboured in Hopcott Brake near Minehead could be found.

True I had not seen them, nor owing to the dry weather and the nature of the soil had I been able to slot them, but the evidence from their " droppings " was so unmistakable as to leave no doubt whatever in my mind that the stags were there. Hopcott Brake, in which I felt certain the stags were lying, has always been known for its most amazingly thick undergrowth of fern. So thick was it that in parts we were scarcely able to ride through it. With no scent on that day to help them it was also difficult for hounds to hunt. When after much labour we had drawn the covert from end to end without finding the slightest sign of a stag, Sidney Tucker declared his belief in no uncertain language that no stags were there. I, on the contrary, continued to maintain there were, so we compromised by enlisting the help of several other horsemen and riding all through the wood again. In spite of making the search as thorough as we possibly could we drew blank. None of the tufters gave so much as a whimper, and Sidney, vowing the deer must have shifted, took his hounds out of the wood and went off to acquaint the Master of the result. Nettled at the turn things were taking, I determined to ride through the wood again on my own, and Mr. James Ridler of Blackford, an old friend and an experienced stag-hunter, kindly volunteered to accompany me. Together we started on what, with no tufters to help us, must have appeared to onlookers an almost

59

ridiculous quest. Luck was, however, with us, for, when we had got almost half-way through the wood, I stopped my horse close by the side of a large holly bush to examine what looked like a kind of tunnel running under the fern. Bending low in the saddle and peering into it I was rewarded by catching sight of an unmistakable glimpse of an antler. I beckoned my companion to the spot and pointed it out to him. With some difficulty he suppressed a desire to " halloa," and we quietly turned our horses' heads away and rode out of the wood.

By this time the Master and huntsman were conferring as to what should be done next.

" A bad job, I'm afraid, Fred," was Lord Bayford's greeting as I approached him. " We must try to give this big field a gallop if we can. Where do you think we can find a stag ? "

" In the wood where we've just been tufting, sir," was my glad reply. " I've just seen one ' sitting ' there."

On this the tufters were quickly put to work again, and on coming to the holly bush, close to which horsemen and hounds must have passed and repassed that morning, a large stag got up.

By what trifling circumstances a closely lying stag may sometimes be discovered is shown by an occasion on which one was betrayed by flies. The meet was at Hawkridge and I had harboured a stag in Church Wood. After a lot of tufting to and fro without any result I thought I would see if I could find the stag in the ditch outside the covert fence. We had previously been up the parallel ditch inside the fence, but had not explored the outer one. The ferns and brambles were very thick and formed a roof over the ditch in a way that made it very difficult to see anything. As I was riding along and peering through the undergrowth I became aware of an enormous swarm of flies buzzing round the brambles at one particular spot. Thinking there must be a reason for this I clambered down the bank and beat the undergrowth with my hunting whip. Thereupon up sprang the stag and leaping the fence nearly jumped right over the huntsman who was riding along the ditch inside.

If deer could tell us what in the whole course of their lives they most dislike I fancy they would say " flies." They are perpetually tormented by them, and in the summer when the " velvet " on the antlers is excessively tender and liable to bleed on the slightest touch, their torture must at times be great. One of the friendliest acts I ever saw performed between one creature and another occurred in connection with flies. When harbouring on Dunkery one morning I was watching a stag lying in the fern on Cloutsham Ball. Through my glasses I could see every detail of his antlers perfectly, and round them were swarming myriads of flies that literally made the air black with their presence. In vain the stag kept trying to rid himself of them by angrily shaking his head. They only returned to draw blood from the tender " velvet " in greater numbers than before. What the stag's gratitude must have been can be imagined when from a thorn bush near by a little bird suddenly flew out and settling on the stag's antlers began to attack the flies. A few snaps with its beak and it was back to the bush again, returning time and again to perch on the antlers and feast on the flies as before. Whether this opportune act sufficed to give any real relief I cannot say, but it was one of the prettiest and friendliest gestures between a bird and a beast that I have ever witnessed, and one I have never seen happen before or since.

Another difficulty in driving the right stag out of a wood occurs from the way large stags have of making younger stags and hinds leave before themselves. Where they do not go of their own accord an old stag will endeavour to drive them out while he still endeavours to remain sheltered. A lucky guess on my part of the number of hinds that would leave a wood we were drawing before the stag moved, resulted in the gift from Lord Bayford of a fine stag's head which I very greatly prize. The meet was at Haddon and I had slotted one good stag and a very considerable number of hinds into West Hill Wood.

" There'll be about twenty hinds come out first," I observed to the Master as I was about to go into the wood with Sidney Tucker and the tufters. One after the other, sure enough, hinds kept on leaving, and after this had gone on for some time without any signs of the stag, I rode out of the wood to see what was happening.

" That's the twentieth hind, Fred," said the Master to me as he pointed to a deer that had just gone by. " Now where's your stag ? " I rejoined the huntsman in the wood and almost imme-diately afterwards we came upon the stag, facing us in one of the rides. For my lucky prediction of the number of hinds I was presented with the head.

Those who find tufting a lengthy process will be interested to learn that from all accounts it is quicker than it used to be in olden times. The larger number of stags has for a long time back made it imperative to isolate one as quickly as possible from the rest. A factor that has largely contributed to this possibility has been " closer harbouring," made available partly by improved field-glasses and partly by more exact knowledge

63

of the whereabouts in woods deer like to lie. Stags not only have a liking for certain woods, but they extend their preference to a particular part of a wood and with experience of this it is often feasible to take the tufters up to the deer without unnecessary waste of time. Likewise in the hunt itself the pace has tended to get faster. In olden days it used to be customary to ride hunters of about fifteen hands, but the combined and public-spirited action of West Country Masters of Stag and Foxhounds in introducing thoroughbred stallions for which farmers over whose land the hunt passes could obtain free nominations, has changed that and made available the faster and better-class hunters ridden to-day. Like all improvements even this has brought disadvantages to some. No longer do all and sundry sportsmen along the countryside—and thorough sportsmen they are too—find it so easy to jump on the back of the first nag they can find, when the hunt chances to come their way, and be in at the kill. In former days the half-bred horses that were used alternately for driving in the gig and farming on the land always turned up on "hunting days." And what with their staying powers and the skill their riders showed in negotiating difficult country they were frequently in at the end of some of the longest runs.

MEMORIES OF A STAG HARBOURER

The late Mr. Jim Bawden of Hawkridge, the father of Ernest Bawden the present huntsman, used to relate with great glee how, as a young man, he was ploughing his father's land one day when hounds unexpectedly came along. Caught up by the enthusiasm he hastily unharnessed his horse from the plough and jumping on it rode bareback in the chase that passed through thirteen parishes to find himself in at the kill! The stag was roused in Upton Wood on 1st October 1852, and ran through the following thirteen parishes, viz.: Upton, King's Brompton, Withiel, Treborough, Luxborough, Exton, Winsford, Exford, Withypool, Hawkridge, East Anstey, Dulverton, and Brushford.*

On another occasion the late Mr. R. S. Westcott of Hawkridge rode barebacked and in his shirt sleeves in the chase through twelve parishes. The deer was found above Northmoor House on 22nd September 1871, and eventually killed at Dry Hill, Stoodleigh, at 8.30 p.m.†

* See *Chase of the Wild Red Deer* (Appendix) by Charles Palk Collyns.

† See *Hunting on Exmoor*, p. 231, by Hon. John Fortescue.

CHAPTER V　　SOME SLOTTING EPISODES

The Barle Valley: Withypool: Hawkridge: Hunting families: Tarr
Steps: A famous run: Difficult harbouring: A long trail: Stag in a
hedgerow: Slotting episode in Syndercombe Valley: Additional signs.

FROM Dulverton upwards the beautiful and thickly
wooded valley of the Barle has always been noted
for deer. At the upper end where the woods give
on to the open moor lies the ancient village of
Withypool, and only a little way below stands
Hawkridge, famous for providing some of the best
sport on the Dulverton side of the moor, as well as
some of the most picturesque scenery. Here it is
that the peculiar stone causeway known as Tarr
Steps crosses the river. Its origin has never been
satisfactorily explained. The popular idea of its
origin gives Satan the credit of bringing the stones
there for a bet. It has also been regarded as the
remains of an old British track across the moor,
but of this MacDermot* says, " it seems to be the
only spot where the line is not largely a matter of
imagination."

From time immemorial, Hawkridge folk have
been staunch stag-hunters. To mention among
others the names of Westcotts and Bawdens is to
recall families who for generations past have given
the Hunt unstinted support, and many are the
kindnesses I have received from them when har-

* *History of the Forest of Exmoor.*

66

bouring. In Gilbert Sloley, recently one of the Whips, son of that good sportsman William Sloley of Hollowcombe Farm, and many others like him, the younger generation of sportsmen follows on.

Between Hawkridge and Dulverton the well-timbered hills that rise steeply on both banks of the river give deer all the seclusion they desire. With' this there is plenty of good food obtainable from the farms near by, and ample means for escape over Winsford Hill on one side and Anstey Common on the other should it be required. That deer are attracted by such pleasant surroundings is not to be wondered at, and many are the famous runs that have started from Hawkridge meets. It was there hounds met to hunt the stag with the seventeen points and undersized slots which for so long deceived me. From there, again, started on 14th September 1899 what has been described by Mr. Philip Everard as " a run of half a century,"* in which many who took part will doubtless like to recall. The harbouring for that day was easy, for any amount of slots and a disorganised turnip field called Devil's Breach on Hawkridge Ridge showed there were plenty of deer about. These deer I had no difficulty in slotting into some oak scrub known as Webbers Plantation, which adjoins

* *Stag-hunting with the Devon and Somerset.*

67

a large wood called Whiterocks, just where the Danesbrook falls into the Barle about half a mile below Hawkridge.

None of the deer I had slotted appeared to be more than five years old, and when the tufters went into the wood a small herd of them soon scuttled out. A nice-looking stag with two-on-top was singled out from the rest, and after the tufters had been stopped the pack was laid on for what proved to be one of the finest runs I can ever remember. So great was the pace, says Mr. Philip Everard in his graphic description of the chase, that for the first two hours over the open moor even the best-conditioned horses had all they could do to live with hounds. Straight from point to point, with no steep ascents, only two small coverts between North Barton Wood and Cheriton were touched, and of a Field of about a hundred that started less than twenty were in at the finish. Nearing Lynton the stag took a path along the cliffs to Glenthorne, where he finally met his end.

For one day in which harbouring is easy there are many when it is difficult. Of these there comes to my mind the memory of a meet at Yard Down, when for slotting deer over a long distance I have never had a similar experience. On taking a look round according to my usual custom in the

afternoon of the day before the meet, I saw unmistakable signs that two stags had recently been
feeding in a field of corn just above Reepham
Wood, low down in the Bray Valley. From the
number of old slots that were about it looked as
though the stags had been in the neighbourhood for
weeks, and I went to bed that night with no
thought of not finding them there in the morning.
Whether something had occurred to make them
suspicious I do not know, but when I went out
soon after daybreak, as I thought just to confirm
their presence by slotting them into the wood, I
found to my surprise they were no longer there.
By that time it was too late to think of harbouring
elsewhere, and my only chance lay in trying to find
out where the stags had gone. I made my first
cast up the Bray turnpike road by the clump of
rocks known as " Lion's Rump," and there I came
upon slots that told me both deer had crossed the
road and gone into Hunstone Wood. On I went
after them, only to find they had passed right
through the wood and taken a line in the direction
of North Molton coverts. Keeping in touch with
their slots and cutting off corners to save time
whenever possible, I followed the line down to the
edge of the stream that runs from Stonybridge to
South Molton Station. By good luck the water
was very low, and here and there long stretches

of sand in the river-bed stood out high and dry. On examining these stretches of sand I saw slots which showed that my two friends had gone upstream.

For about a mile and a half I followed them up the river-bed by picking out slots here and there on the sand. On approaching North Molton the tracks broke away from the water-course, and continuing over Oakford Farm towards Bampfylde Clump they eventually led me on to the North Molton—Yard Down road. There they crossed and went on to Lord Poltimore's Home Coverts.

Realising there would be now no possibility of my getting back to Yard Down in time for the meet I left the line at this juncture and rode into North Molton. From there I sent a telegram to Earl Fortescue at Simonsbath, whose residence I knew the hounds would be passing, to ask that the pack might be brought on to North Molton. I then returned to my harbouring, and picking up the slots again where I had left them I followed the tracks into Old Park Wood, where I flattered myself my work would end. Making a cast in such a way as to be sure the stags had not crossed the drive at the bottom, to my great disappointment I found they had crossed by the young plantation and still gone on. Through this plantation and across the meadows beyond I still followed the slots which took me straight up to South Wood, where the journey at last ended. A good breakfast at Court Hall, and by that time it was about a quarter to twelve and the hounds had arrived.

The tufters soon got to work and put the two stags up. They were lying close to each other, and both got up at the same time. After circling once or twice round the wood together, one broke away. The pack was then laid on, and after a good run in which the stag took the hounds back over the same line along which I had slotted him that morning he eventually escaped. This is considerably the longest distance slotting I have ever accomplished, and but for Mr. John Robins of Lydcot Farm who kindly came to my assistance and led my horse while I was engaged in slotting the deer up the stream and in other inaccessible places, it is more than doubtful if I should ever have succeeded in coming up with the deer in time.

A stag I once thought I had harboured for a meet at Brendon Two Gates played me a very similar trick. From the disordered state of a mangold field which I saw in the afternoon I had no doubt about harbouring a stag in Barton Wood the next morning. So certain did I feel about it that I did not go round to the mangold field to see if he had been on the feed again till well after daylight, and then to my annoyance I found the stag had not been there. As at Yard Down I had to hunt round the wood to see which way he had gone. Before long I found slots which showed the deer had jumped out of Barton Wood on to the road leading from Hillsford Bridges to Scob Hill Gate. After continuing along the road as far as Brendon Manor the slots took an abrupt turn which indicated the deer had jumped over the road-side wire fence and gone in the direction of Church Wood which adjoins Farley Wood. Thinking that would be the stag's final destination, for it is a wood in which deer like to lie, I cast round the boundaries only to find the slots were skirting the wood and not leading into it. On I went until the trail took me to another mangold field on Farley Farm, where it was obvious the stag had recently been feeding. As the stag was clearly not in the mangold field my idea was that he must have gone on to Farley Combe or towards Badgworthy. Accordingly I cast for slots up Farley Lane and along the beech fence that borders the moor to Scob Hill Gate. Try as I would, no slots could I find and it now began to be a mystery where the stag could have gone. Thinking there must be slots somewhere I made another cast, and this time I completely encircled the mangold field at about two fields' distance from it. Still no slots were anywhere to be seen. Finally I came to the conclusion that the only place in which the stag could be lying was in the very ordinary thorny hedge separating the field of mangolds from the field next to it. The slots of this deer were of the " shell " variety, in which only the outline shows, as described on page 44. There was thus very little to be seen, and the fact that it was dry weather made the impressions on the hard ground still fainter.

In these circumstances the decision that the stag was lying in such an unusual place as an ordinary hedgerow separating two fields took some making, but taking my courage in both hands I met the hounds at Scob Hill Gate and told the Master the conclusion at which I had arrived. On hearing what I had to say the Master decided to draw with the pack. Thereupon hounds were brought to the spot, and proceeded to draw the hedgerow upwards in the direction of the moor. The huntsman and I rode one side of the fence while the Whip rode up the other. Nothing happened until we were about half-way along, when suddenly the hounds began to draw inwards with their sterns back like pointers, and a few seconds later they put up a big stag with four-on-top. Away he went right across the moor. The hounds were then stopped and after a short time were laid on again, eventually to come up with their stag at Brendon.

This is the only occasion in the whole of my experience that I ever harboured a stag in an ordinary hedgerow between two fields.

A morning's harbouring full of interesting slotting episodes occurred one day when I was at Syndercombe Valley in the neighbourhood of North Molton. On the preliminary round the day before the meet, I saw that two or three stags had been feeding in a field of corn and young grass at the top of the wood. This was a very favourite wood for deer, and no difficulty in harbouring was expected. On account of the height of the hedges there was no spot from which I could hope to view deer, so off I went next morning just after daylight to the cornfield again to see if there were any fresh slots. The slots were there all right, and just before the stags had left the field the irregular way the toes of the slots had been stuck into the ground and the way the imprints were scattered about showed the deer had been sparring and frisking about. In acting thus they had crushed some wild mint that was growing freely at the edge of the field, and the smell coming from the crushed leaves was so fresh and strong that very little time could have passed since the stags had been there. Had the ground been such as to make slotting difficult, the fresh smell of mint would by itself have been sufficient to tell me the stags had been lately there. As it happened the slotting was so far easy and took me out of the field and into the adjacent wood. Eight times out of ten I would have put my money on the stags staying in that wood, but on casting round the wood I found this was one of the exceptions, for by their slots I saw the stags had come out again and gone on down to a stream. There my difficulties began, for it took me half an hour before I could find out whether they had gone up or down. At last at a sharp bend of the stream some distance up, there was a bit of sand on which I found slots showing the deer had walked across it in an upward direction. On that I continued to follow the stream up, but saw no further traces of them until I came to a small wood called Higher Ley Wood, where slots showed the deer had sprung from the water on to the bank, and then gone into the wood. There, fortunately for me they had remained, and there they still were when the hounds came to rouse them later on.

At such times as slots are not available either on account of the rain filling them up and making it impossible to tell whether they are new or old, or owing to the dryness or stoniness of the soil being so great that no imprints are left on it, other signs must be looked for. On one very wet morning when slotting was difficult I noticed some rape stems, that had been bitten off where deer had been, were still green. The green colour told me the stems could not have been exposed to the hot sun that had been shining the day before, and proved conclusively that the rain-filled slots in the field had been recently made. Droppings sometimes form important guides. From hinds they fall separately and resemble those of a sheep. from stags they fall in clusters and are much bigger. The degree of hardness and dryness of droppings afford indications of their freshness or otherwise.

Antlers: Annual shedding: Effects on stags: Method and rapidity of growth: "Velvet": Influence on nutrition: Appearance of various antler points in accordance with age: "All his rights": "Going back": Variations: Irregular growths: Freaks: "Nott" stags: A three-horned stag: Death through deformity of antler: An entanglement: Characters of a "good head": The St. Audries head: History in "heads."

THE beauty of a stag lies largely in its antlers or "beamed frontlet," technically known as the "head."

Antlers are commonly referred to as "horns" but they have nothing in common in their growth with the horny substance proper that adorns the heads of sheep, cows and other kindred cattle.

Unlike true horns which gradually grow to their required size, antlers are shed ("mewed") and renewed every year. Every April or thereabouts, the date being rather later for younger stags than for older ones, the antlers drop off. This happens without any apparent preliminary change and quite irrespective of where the animal chances to be or what it may be doing. It occurs sometimes while the deer is quietly feeding or at other times while it is jumping a fence, or the antlers may be found where the deer has been lying. Both antlers may come off at the same time or one may drop off before the other but in the latter case the second antler usually falls off very soon after the first. I have seen antlers actually falling from some of the stags on Haddon, and I have picked them up in all sorts of places. On one occasion the two horns were lying across each other and had probably fallen off simultaneously. At other times I have picked them up a mile or so apart. By those who are constantly about the woods cast off antlers are frequently picked up, but they are by no means easy to find by design. In former times a fair price could always be obtained from visitors for a good pair, and quite a number of people consequently used to spend a lot of time in looking for them. Latterly, the demand has for some reason or other not been so great. There is a belief prevalent among some of the experienced observers of deer in Scotland that shed antlers are eaten by hinds, but I have never seen any evidence of it in this part of the country. I think myself the explanation of the difficulty in finding shed antlers lies in the fact that they are shed just about the season that bracken and other kinds of undergrowth are beginning to shoot up. They are thus effectually hidden in spring, and buried under the falling leaves and decaying undergrowth in autumn.

Tenderness of the stumps that follows the shedding process causes the deer to retire to the most secluded parts of the woods and moor as soon as the antlers drop off. In this way they not only avoid branches and other objects coming into contact with their tender heads, but they also escape the bullying attention, of younger deer whose antlers fall off at a rather later date. I have an idea that their heads begin to feel sore a little while before the shedding occurs, but of this I have no actual proof.

During the first twelve months of its life the male deer has no antlers, but occupies the time in growing the pedicles from which the antlers will eventually spring. These pedicles are direct outgrowths from the frontal bones of the skull with which they remain continuous, and after passing through a period during which they are of pulpy consistency they settle down into hard bone. Once fully formed, the pedicles are permanent, growing in circumference every year to meet the requirements of larger and larger antlers, and then " going back " as the antlers start to deteriorate with oncoming old age.

From the " cup " on each of the pedicles the antlers grow with a rapidity practically unknown for any other normal structures. Bereft of antlers in April, or in the case of younger stags in May, the new ones are by the following September fully matured. During their growth the antlers derive the requisite nutrition chiefly from a finely constructed covering called the " velvet." In the

79

meshwork of the velvet, which is exceedingly sensitive and bleeds on the slightest touch, run the tiny nerves and blood-vessels that administer to the growth. It is this tender membrane that the deer are so anxious to shield by hiding themselves away in quiet spots as soon as the last year's antlers are shed. The instinct that prompts them to avoid painful knocks at this period serves to promote regularity in growth, for any injury to the velvet is liable to be followed by a permanent scar or deformity in the corresponding part of the antler for that year.

Also, as I have already mentioned, the old stags by hiding away, avoid the indignities which the three-year-olds that retain their antlers to a later date are always ready to shower on them. Finding themselves suddenly masters of the situation these younger stags lose no time in showing off their superior butting powers, and I have at those times seen many a youngster puffed out with a pride that would three weeks sooner quickly have had a fall. Towards the end of July the growth of the antlers is completed and the hardening process begins to set in. This starts at the bottom and extends upwards until the whole of the antler assumes the density of hard bone. With the hardening finished off, the velvet has served its purpose and is no longer required. It thereupon begins to wither and shrivel up, and, round about the 20th of August, the stags finding they have no further use for it, start to "clean" their horns by rubbing it off. This they do by rubbing the antlers against trees ("fraying"), and then is the time that withy bushes and other trees they find convenient for the purpose suffer. Within a few days of the time the velvet starts to shrivel it is all gone, and by the beginning of September there are few antlers that are not clear of it. Up to a certain age of the deer, additional points should grow on every new set of antlers, but their number and size depend to a considerable extent on the quality of the feed and health of the deer, and its freedom from any kind of injury.

Other things being equal, calves of well-nourished mothers have a better start in life than those of mothers less well fed. Stag for stag, one living in the vicinity of farms in the enclosed parts of the country is more likely to grow a bigger head than one seeking a more precarious existence on the open moor. A hard winter in the earlier years of life, with snow lying on the hills perhaps for six weeks or more as it sometimes does, often puts a deer in a different category from those that have known only green winters and plenty of food. In winters of prolonged severity deer may be hard put to it to find a meal. I have seen them standing disconsolately with arched backs and feet close together, scraping away the snow on Dunkery in the hope of finding a few heather tops. At other times they are thankful for a patch of ivy leaves or may be some bramble leaves that have outlasted their fellows in a sheltered place. All of which is in strange contrast with the corn and turnip fields they go through so freely in more propitious times.

Within certain averages the following are the lines along which antlers usually develop.

Up to the age of twelve months the male deer has no antlers, but in preparation for them grows the pedicles already described. During the next twelve months two " uprights " or " spires " spring up which by the August succeeding the deer's first birthday are from nine to twelve inches long. In the twelve months following, two lateral branches, known as " points " or " tines " grow out from each of the uprights. These are the " brow " and " tray " points. The deer therefore during his third year should possess brow and tray points and an upright on each side. By this time also the whole head has begun to assume the curve or " spread " that for the future increases each year.

In his fourth year the deer should have acquired

another point on top, making brow and tray with two on top each side. During the next twelve months the coveted " bay " point should appear, so that in his fifth year the deer should be the proud possessor of what is known as " all his rights," *i.e.* brow, bay, and tray points with two points on top each side. From now onwards he is promoted to the title of stag, having hitherto only been known as a young male deer. The bay tine grows between the brow and the tray. It by no means always appears, and sometimes it is present on one side and not on the other. When it is absent there is sometimes an extra point on top to make up for it, and thus the stag may have brow, bay, tray and two on top on one side, and brow, tray and three on top on the other side. At six years the stag should have another point on top, thus giving him " all his rights," and three on top each side. With the growth of additional points which get longer and sharper each year the " beam " and spread of the antlers continues to increase in mass and curve until maximum growth is finally attained. Between the age of six and nine more points may be added on top and the beam become weightier, but otherwise there is not much change. They are the years in which the West Country stag is at its best. After the age of nine signs of advancing years begin to creep on, and with this the antlers begin to go back. The points which have been increasing in number and improving in quality up to the prime of life now begin to get fewer while those remaining become blunter and sometimes the tops become bifurcated at their ends. I have known stags to go right back in their old age to brow, tray and uprights, a veritable return to second childhood!

While it is generally possible to estimate the approximate age of a stag fairly closely by its antlers up to the age of eight or nine, it must be admitted there are many exceptions.

Illness or accident may easily cause the absence of a point or two on top, and in these cases the beam will also probably be smaller than it should be. I have known six-year-old stags to have only two points on top and never to get any more, and in a few instances although they have possessed brow, bay and tray, they have only carried their uprights, without any branching. In the event of this latter occurrence the absence of points on top is often compensated by the possession of bigger beams and longer and stronger brow points. Besides all such variations as these, there are irregular growths and " freaks " to be taken into account. Some stags have no horns at all or possibly only two large knobs where the horns should be. These hornless ones are known as

" Nott " stags, and by inexperienced observers are often taken for hinds. They frequently grow into big animals. I have known a good many. There was one in Haddon that I watched growing up over several years.

Others I can call to mind were to be seen at Cloutsham, Culbone, and Hawkcombe Head. The one at Hawkcombe Head I eventually harboured and he met his end at Oare. In the absence of horns, the Nott stag makes no attempt to use his head for butting, but will fight furiously with his feet. As a class I do not consider Nott stags run very well. There are, however, exceptions, and a big one whose existence had long been known to the Hunt was roused and killed in 1896 after showing " such sport as will long be remembered."*

There are deer that possess only one horn, and of these I have known a great many.

Not very long ago one was found in Haddon with a single horn only about nine inches long growing downwards by the side of the face. He gave the hounds a good run, and from the appearance of the teeth and slots was judged to be about seven years old.

Various other irregularities are met with from time to time. Among the more curious of these was a stag that had lost the sight of an eye, through

* *Stag-hunting with the Devon and Somerset.*

a point on one of the antlers projecting downwards and destroying the sight. This stag was often in the Haddon Woods, and I knew him as well as anything. He was hunted more than once, but being an adept at changing places with other deer whenever hard pressed he several times managed to escape.

The irregular growth had probably resulted from a local injury to the growing antler while still soft and while the velvet was still on, as it did not recur in the antlers of subsequent years. When the deer was eventually killed the antler deformity was no longer present, but the loss of the eye of course remained.

The only stag I have ever seen with three horns * I harboured on Winsford Allotments in 1901. He was lying not much more than three hundred yards from a spot where the hounds were to meet. I reported to Lord Bayford that I had harboured a stag with three horns, and thereupon he came with the tufters in order to see it. We went straight up to the fern bed where I knew the stag was lying and the Master and Sidney Tucker and I all stood within a few yards of the stag and looked at him. He proved to be a stag of some

* The stag killed on the day that King Edward hunted with the Devon and Somerset, 22nd August 1879, had on the off side brow, tray and upright, and on the near three long single points, each growing separately from the skull.—Mr. Bisset's *Diary*.

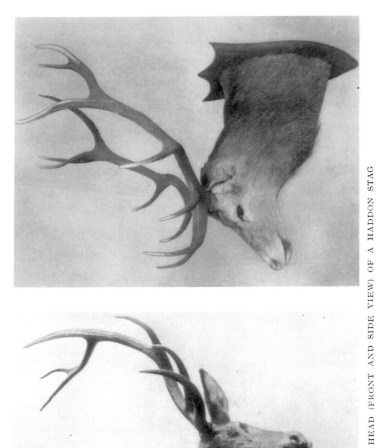

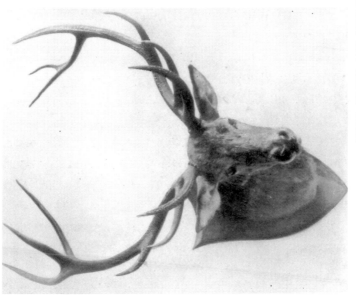

HEAD (FRONT AND SIDE VIEW) OF A HADDON STAG

seven or eight years of age. There was, I believe, some question as to whether the third stem grew from the normal beam or whether it was an entirely independent antler, which I fancy it was eventually considered to be. I had never seen this particular deer before that day, and it is the only instance of a stag having three horns that I have met with. I have occasionally seen a brow point forked at the end, and the same sort of thing I have known also to occur in a bay and a tray. One stag I knew grew on one side a good brow, bay and tray with three-on-top, while on the other side there was nothing more than a simple long horn dividing into two close to the base.

I know of a stag at the present time that I often see in Haddon, with brow, bay, tray and three-on-top on one side and on the other side only brow, tray and upright. Surprise is sometimes expressed that antlers never seem to obstruct the rapidity of a stag's movements in woods, but with their noses thrust upwards and their horns lying back almost in line with the body, stags cleverly incline the head from side to side and glide unhindered through the densest parts. Antlers may, however, occasionally lead their owner into trouble. One stag I knew came by his death in this way, through the unusual formation of one of his points-on-top. Points-on-top generally grow in what we in the West Country call " brandish " fashion, *i.e.* after the shape of a brandish, which is a tripod stand on which to put a frying-pan, and is still used on the hearth fires in many farm-houses. Instances have come to my notice in which, instead of the points growing in this usual fashion, one of them has grown projected almost directly backwards with a long downward curve, and this was the case in the stag to which I now allude. He was a big stag and one which on account of this peculiar point I knew by sight quite well. He had also to my knowledge been hunted two or three times, but had always managed to escape.

After the stag-hunting season for that year was over I was one day riding through Higher Stockham Wood looking for hinds when I saw what I took to be a deer crouching on the ground about twenty yards below the path. On going up to it I found it had evidently been dead for some long time. It was lying close up against a partially uprooted tree of large size, some of the roots of which were still firmly embedded in the ground. Further investigation showed the stag had been using one of the firmly embedded roots as a " fraying stock " against which to rub his horns. In doing this he had evidently managed to get the long backwardly directed crook under the root where it was still securely hooked up. The root was too strong and thick to break, and the angle at which it came off from the partially uprooted trunk was such as to leave insufficient space for the stag to get under it. With careful manipulation it is probable the stag could have extricated himself, but the clumsy and frightened struggles which no doubt ensued availed him nothing, and the wretched animal must have died a miserable death.

When tufting with Sidney Tucker one day in Berry Hill Wood close to Leeworthy Bridge for a Yard Down meet, we saw a stag with something clinging to its horns. It looked in the distance like pieces of rope, and on account of this peculiarity we picked out the stag to hunt in preference to several other equally good ones that were about. When the end came after a good run, we found the entanglement to be an ordinary pig net such as farmers are in the habit of putting over the tops of their carts when taking pigs to market. How the deer picked it up we never knew, but from the appearances the net seemed to have been on the horns for quite a long time.

To possess a good head a stag should have " all his rights," and at least three-on-top each side. The beam should be of large size with a long, symmetrical curve. Large heads are very heavy. I have known them to weigh nine pounds, which is a good weight for our West Country deer. I think the biggest head I ever saw was on a stag I harboured in the Winsford Allotments for Lord Bayford. It had seventeen points and was not unlike the other one with seventeen points and undersized slots that I harboured during the same season. It was a fine head, though two others possessed by Colonel Wiggin, in one of which the points are possibly longer, are nearly if not quite its equal. The finest head recorded in the West Country is said to be the " St. Audries Head." The stag was killed at the end of the 1893 season. It had four-on-top at one side, and four and an " offer " on the other with a very large and finely curved beam.

The history of the " Devon and Somerset " is largely written in the heads that adorn the country seats around. At Castle Hill, Holnicote, Pixton, Baron's Down, Bayford Lodge, and Stockleigh Lodge, the heads that adorn the walls and those of many other country seats bring home to us the distinction and antiquity of stag-hunting with a sense of reality scarcely possible in any other way.

CHAPTER VII   HIND AND STAG HUNTING

Hind-hunting: Season: Harbouring not usually necessary: Tufting: The "lay-on": Comparison with stags: A good run: Spring stag-hunting: Preference for young stags: Some long runs.

THE season for hunting hinds starts at the beginning of November and lasts up to the end of February. All hinds over two years of age are considered huntable, and as there is no difficulty to the experienced eye in picking out one that is old enough, the necessity for harbouring any particular hind beforehand as in the case of a stag does not arise. There are, however, some districts in which hinds are apt to be scarce, as for instance, Woolhanger, The Chains, and Yard Down, and when meets are being held in those parts it is as well to have some knowledge beforehand where the deer are to be found. This information, as in the case of a stag, is obtained either by seeing the hinds in the open or by slotting them into a wood. Hinds are usually found in herds, and the initial difficulty in hunting them is to separate one of them from the rest. As in hunting stags a start is made with tufters, but on account of the difficulty often encountered in getting a hind away from the herd, as many as six to eight couples of hounds are generally used for this purpose. Once a hind has been driven out of the wood it is necessary to keep her on the move or she will quickly rejoin the herd, and once she is mixed up with them the procedure has to begin all over again. For the same reason the tufters are not so definitely stopped before the pack is laid on as they are in stag-hunting. The lay on is altogether less formal and dependent largely on a convenient moment. What generally happens is that the second horseman in charge of the pack brings the pack on behind and awaits his opportunity to hand the hounds over to the huntsman at such time as the latter judges it best to lay on.

For the huntsman, hind-hunting is very hard work on account of the continual likelihood of changing deer. Unlike the comparative ease with which one stag can be distinguished from another by the antlers, the general similarity between one hind and another is so close that great care and experience are required to know if the hounds are keeping to the same deer. Hinds are fleeter of foot and much tougher than stags. They will often run for three or four hours without showing any signs of fatigue. The short winter days when they are hunted and the heavy rains that so often make rivers impassable for horses at that time of year are all in favour of the hind. Add to these handicaps a fog making distant vision difficult or a frost to hinder the pace, and it becomes understandable that hounds not infrequently return home without venison.

Hinds are less inclined to go straight across country in spite of the many hours they often run. A stag generally makes for a certain point, and unlike a fox does not allow the direction of the wind to influence his decision. Hinds, on the other hand, are more likely to take a roundabout course in and out of coverts, round commons and back again rather than make up their minds to go for a definite point. There are of course plenty of exceptions in which long cross-country runs have occurred, especially after Christmas. I remember one we found in Hele Ball Wood above Jury, close to Dulverton, that ran to Milverton before being killed—a run of a good many miles. This run was with Sir John Amory's Stag-hounds, and Mr. Albert Las Casas, who usually acted as Honorary Whip, was hunting them on that day in the place of the Master who was ill.

After the season for hunting hinds is over, as it is about the end of February, the hounds are given a short rest before beginning spring stag-hunting. Spring stag-hunting was introduced when the late Mr. Basset was Master. It starts at the beginning of April and goes on for about a month. When the spring season was first inaugurated big stags were hunted like they are in the autumn. During the time Lord Bayford was Master it was decided to hunt three and four-year-olds in preference to the big ones, since the latter being almost about to shed their horns are not in such good condition as the younger ones which shed their horns rather later.

These younger deer—three and four-year-olds —are very active and difficult for hounds to come up with, and frequently afford very good runs.

The run from Crowcombe Heathfield to the River Exe at Winsford, referred to in Chapter XV, was given by a spring stag. Another run was from Reepham Wood in the Bray Valley to Dulverton, and many others equally good that the spring stags have given could be quoted, notably that of 18th April 1931, when they ran from Reepham Wood to the Chain's Hoar Oak, Badgworthy, Weir Wood, Nutscale, Pitsworthy, Exford and through Court Wood to the Exe at Hantons. This stag had a very peculiar head— though at least four years old he carried an upright on the off side and a somewhat longer horn, also devoid of points, projecting at right angles on the near.

THE district of Haddon, through the valley of which runs the River Haddeo, covers a large area of the upper part of the Pixton estate. On it are several hundreds of acres of moorland and woods, some of the latter extending for miles. Beyond the Haddon woods come the Bittiscombe woods owned by Sir Henry Ferguson-Davie, and beyond these again is the well-wooded Bulland estate belonging to Mr. Capel. These properties, on both of which deer are strictly preserved, afford in conjunction with Haddon a very large and practically continuous area for deer to roam in.

Deer have a decided preference for some woods over others. Stags are particularly fond of Haddon Wood and Storridge Wood which cover the hills on either side of the Haddeo Valley between Bury and Hartford. Hinds on the other hand show a decided preference for the wooded district known as the " Deer park " higher up the valley. This so-called " Deer park " takes its name solely from the fact that deer are nearly always there in plenty, and is in no sense an enclosure of any kind. With plenty of good food easily obtainable from the farms around, Haddon stags have, generally speaking, somewhat bigger heads than those living on Exmoor where in winter time scarcity of food and want of shelter are both often considerable. Though the Haddon stag is, on account of the great size of the woods, difficult to get away, for which reason the locality is not altogether a favourite one for meets, once the stag is clear of the coverts he will run as far as any other. The first one I ever harboured for a meet took the hounds for some eighteen miles and still lived to repeat the performance three weeks later. Others, in going to Dunster, Washford, Wheal Eliza on the Barle below Simonsbath, and suchlike distant places, have many times furnished the Hunt with runs equal to any obtainable elsewhere.

Except for occasional meets of the Stag-hounds, wild life on Haddon was in my early days there very little disturbed. Foxes were particularly plentiful, but on account of the numbers of deer and the great size of the woods they were very seldom hunted. The fifth Earl Portsmouth who died in 1891 and Mr. Froude Bellew of Rhyll, East Anstey, had occasionally brought hounds there, but that was before my day, and it was not until I had been harbourer and keeper for about six years that I first saw a fox hunted there. Even then the meet was not part of the set programme, but arose out of a chance meeting between Mr. Jasper Selwyn, at that time Master of the Dulverton Fox-hounds, and myself.

" Any foxes in Haddon, Fred ? " he asked jocularly, as he generally did whenever I happened to meet him.

" Plenty," I replied. " Why don't you bring your hounds up sometimes ? "

" Too many deer," was the answer.

" But you've never been to try," I protested. " Come up and see."

" All right. We'll come on such and such a day," he replied, consulting his pocket diary and mentioning a date. " But," he added, laughing, " you'll have to harbour a fox for us."

On the day before the hounds were due to come, it rained so heavily that it became advisable to release the sluice gates of a water-course used for irrigating a meadow at the bottom of Haddon Hill. In doing this I got so wet that no sooner had I finished than I made a bee-line across the heather for home instead of going up the hill by the path. On my way I passed a solitary young Scotch fir, and within three or four yards of this convenient landmark a fine fox got up just in front of me. The place where he had been lying under

G 97

the heather was carefully hollowed out, and looked
as if it had been used for many along day. Making
a mental note of the position, I went on. The
following morning the rain had ceased and the sun
was shining brightly when in the best of spirits
the Hunt met with the hope of a good run.

" Well, Fred, have you harboured that fox for
us ? " was the Master's greeting.

" Yes. That's quite all right," I replied. Then
pointing out the little fir tree which was plainly
visible from where we were standing, I said,
" You'll find your fox under that tree."

The Master at first looked somewhat doubtful
as to whether this was to be taken seriously, but
as I volunteered no further explanation (nor have
I done so to this day) and he saw I was in earnest,
he directed the huntsman to put my words to the
test.

For a few minutes I wondered if my " spec."
was coming off, and then to my amusement the
fox got up exactly where I said it would be found.
After the kill, which took place at Steart after a
good run round several miles of country, the
Secretary of the Hunt brought the mask over to
me with a message from the Master saying he
would be pleased if I would accept it. This mask,
on the back of which is inscribed " Dulverton Fox
Hounds, April 6, 1900," remains in my possession

to this day as a valued memento of the first fox hunt in which I ever rode—though I have enjoyed many a good run since.

To see foxes out in the open or at play when cubs are about is quite an ordinary event, but it is rare that an opportunity occurs for watching an old fox lying curled up in his bed.

The only occasion on which I have seen one was when trying to harbour a stag on the moor. The morning was very misty and the hour for harbouring was getting uncomfortably late when at last the fog began to lift curtain-like upwards from the ground. I was standing by a withy bush on Trout Hill—a favourite spot of mine from which I had often harboured stags—and lost no time in scanning the landscape around as soon as it was possible to see. Knowing that at so late an hour the deer would be almost sure to have settled down for the day, I directed my glasses on to the fern on the opposite side of Buscombe in the hope of seeing some antlers. A speck of brown caught my attention and on focussing the glasses I found myself looking at a fox lying on the edge of a clump of fern. He was evidently just finishing the morning's ablutions, and was busily engaged in licking his forefeet. One after the other he diligently washed them over, and then curling himself up comfortably under the bracken he settled down to sleep. Had the fox-hounds chanced to be about I could have led them right up to him. Cubs are full of interest to watch. The way they come out of a burrow is most amusing. First the tip of a nose appears and then after a cautious but somewhat perfunctory look round, out dashes the first cub followed helter-skelter by the rest, after which they proceed to roll one another over and bite one another's brushes in the most playful way. An old fox exercises much greater caution before showing himself. Whilst rabbiting I once stood quite close to one that was being bolted by the ferrets. First only the very tip of the nose cautiously showed, and then bit by bit the head and body gradually drew out of the hole until only the hind quarters and brush were still hidden. At that stage of the proceedings I purposely made a noise. For the fraction of a second the fox looked taken aback. Then with a lightning-like rapidity that needs to be seen to be appreciated, he fled through the wood out of sight. Foxes carry their prey in front of them in the same way as a dog, and do not throw geese over their shoulders in the manner depicted in fairy tales in which foxes frequently figure.

The size and variety of the larder a dog fox and vixen will collect when they have cubs is amazing. The following are the items I once came across outside an earth in Storridge Wood : a tiny newly born sucking pig, six mice all stuck together with saliva-like substance into a kind of bundle, a grass snake, a piece of sheep's liver and various remains of pheasants and rabbits, the whole giving off one of the most awful stenches I have ever met with. What especially puzzled me was where the dead sucking pig could have come from, as it was most unlikely any old sow would have tolerated interference with her young. I took the trouble to inquire around Hartford whether any pigs had been missed. It turned out that a farmer in the neighbourhood had recently lost a litter just after they were born, and instead of burying them someone had thrown them into a stream from which they had been washed up on to a sandbank three or four fields lower down. My only conclusion was that it was one of these the fox had found and carried away.

When hard pressed for food, foxes will stop at nothing, as my wife can testify from seeing one enter the fowl house on Haddon in the middle of an afternoon. We had been missing fowls for some time, and on seeing a brownish animal going into the fowl house, which from the momentary glimpse obtained looked to her like a dog, she hurried across the yard and closed the door on it. That was the position of things when I got home, and thinking the captive dog, as I supposed it to be, would rush by me the moment the door was opened, I lifted a loose tile off the fowl-house roof and cautiously looked inside. To my surprise a large fox was running round and round trying to find a way out. He was in a terrible state of mange and the brush except at the tip was almost bare, so that there was nothing for it but to kill him. Though I got the better of this fox, another one once had the laugh on me. One morning when I had to be away early I went to look at some rabbit snares before it was properly light. As I jumped over the fence close to the spot where I knew one of the snares had been set something white showed up on the ground. Taking it to be the white belly of a rabbit I bent down and gripped hold of it to pick it up. The moment I caught hold of it I knew it was not a rabbit, and my feelings can better be imagined than described when I realised I was grasping the white chest of a fox. It gave out an angry spitting and gurgling sound, and I dropped it again in quicker time than it takes to tell. I suppose in taking it up, the noose must have become loosened, for the moment I let go again the animal was off like a shot and fortunately without biting me. I should be sorry to say which was the more frightened, the fox or I.

The worst scare I think I ever had in my time

happened one winter and also in the early morning. While walking along Hartford Bottom before it was light I heard what I took to be a deer rushing through the wood by the roadside. The next moment something heavy pitched on to the road right in front of me, to be followed almost instantaneously by a tremendous crash like the sound of breaking glass. The explanation proved simple. A deer had jumped from the wood on to the road, and scared no doubt at seeing me took another leap and landed in the middle of a large sheet of ice !

To return to foxes. Their craftiness is almost beyond belief. Having been asked by the Master of the Dulverton Hounds if I could get him a litter together with the vixen for turning down in another part of the country, I eventually found one near Wynne Corner on Haddon and proceeded to dig them out. After a good deal of hard work, for the earth was a large one, I came upon nine cubs, but no vixen could anywhere be found. Knowing it was no use sending away cubs of that age by themselves I put them back wondering at the time how one of them that had a crooked neck would get on if it ever came to facing hounds. The next day I went back to see what had happened and found the family had gone, and rather than risk entering the hole around which I had previously been digging the vixen had carefully avoided that route and had bored straight down to her cubs from the top through a fresh hole she made three or four yards above. About six weeks after this I came upon what I thought was another litter of cubs quite a mile and a half away from where I found the first lot, and as I had not yet supplied the Master of Foxhounds with as many as he wanted, I proceeded to dig these out. I found eight alive and well and one dead. Among the living was my little friend with the crooked neck, by which I recognised the litter as the one that had moved house from Wynne Corner. The cubs being now old enough to take care of themselves they were handed over to the Master, and I often wonder how the little chap with the crooked neck fared. I have only once seen newly born cubs laid down on the open ground, and that was when I was on my way to Lyncombe Farm at the top end of Storridge Wood. On crossing the middle of a rough field containing short gorse and heather a fox suddenly jumped out of a patch of gorse almost at my feet. Looking into the place it had sprung from I found to my surprise all huddled together in a little bed nicely made under the gorse nine newly born cubs. They looked very little bigger than moles. In order to count them

I turned one or two of them over with the end of my walking stick, but otherwise left them quite undisturbed. On my return journey two or three hours later I thought I should like to see if the vixen had come back, but on going to the spot I found the whole lot had disappeared. Disturbed no doubt at my having seen her family the vixen had in that short time carried them all away.

Hares also were very plentiful on Haddon when I first went there. Mr. Henson of Morebath used to hunt these with his harriers. As time went on they gradually got scarcer and there are not many to be seen there now. I have already told how ferrets once bolted a fox. Another unusual experience of a similar kind was bolting an otter. It happened in Keen's Wood close to Hartford about two years ago. We were just finishing up, and on finding we had got forty-nine rabbits I suggested getting one more to make the fifty. The ferrets were accordingly put into a burrow on the side of a hill, and about two hundred yards distant from the River Haddeo. About a minute after the ferrets had gone in out came a fine otter. For a moment we could not think what it was, and one of the keepers able only to catch a glimpse of it among the bushes shouted that it was a cat. It quickly, however, came into full view, and dashing down the hillside with a retriever close on its heels took a flying leap into the river below, down which it went with a furrow like that from a boat !

Otters are voracious feeders and eat many things besides fish. One I can vouch for took a moor-hen down almost under my nose at Hele Bridge Weir. I was fishing in the rough water below the Weir at the time, and several moor-hens were swimming to and fro in the smooth weir pool above me. My attention was attracted by a " clucking " noise they were making, and then suddenly one of them began to flutter and struggle on the top of the water. In another moment the bird was drawn under, and a wave showed it being drawn towards the opposite bank. I ran forward to see what had happened, and was just in time to see a big otter with a moor-hen in its mouth disappearing under the stump of a tree.

On looking back I think some of the happiest days in my life were those when harbouring was at its busiest and when hunting seemed at its zenith. It included a period in which in addition to harbouring for the " Devon and Somerset " four days a week, I was often employed in harbouring for Sir John Amory's Stag-hounds on the other two. In this way I have several times harboured six stags in a week. The rate at which deer were increasing in spite of the efforts of Mr. R. A.

Sanders with the " Devon and Somerset " and Mr. E. A. V. Stanley with the Quantock Stag-hounds to keep them down, made it necessary to cope further with them.

The plan of hunting the Tiverton country with the " Devon and Somerset " for a definite period in each year had formerly been made possible by the late Mr. Tom Yandle inviting them to Duvale where horses and hounds were generously put up by him for a week.

This, however, proved insufficient for the purpose, and in 1896 Sir John Amory formed a new pack to hunt, by arrangement with the Master of the " Devon and Somerset," the country south of the railway line between Taunton and Barnstaple. This pack was hunted by the late Sir Ian Amory (then Mr. Ian Amory), and in his absence by Colonel (then Captain) Harry Heathcoat Amory. Meets in the Haddon and other neighbouring districts were often held by invitation of the Master of the " Devon and Somerset," and for these I was generally asked to harbour a stag. Later on, Miller and then Lang, the present harbourer for the " Devon and Somerset," used to harbour for them. When Sir Ian Amory took over the Master-ship of the Tiverton Fox-hounds, Colonel Harry Amory became Master of Sir John Amory's Stag-hounds and kept the hounds at Hele Manor,

Dulverton. On leaving for military service Colonel Harry Amory gave many of his hounds to the " Devon and Somerset," the remainder being looked after and hunted during the difficult war years by Mr. Charles Slader of South Molton. On Mr. Slader giving them up, they became the " Tiverton Stag-hounds " of to-day, passing into the hands of the Yandle family, sons of the late Mr. Tom Yandle, whose keen sportsmanship all the country deeply respected.

I have in my possession a highly valued memento of the five-hundredth deer killed by Sir John Amory's pack, in the form of one of the stag's tusks mounted as a safety pin.

And also another happy reminder of this period in the shape of a silver-mounted blotter presented to me by Sir Ian Amory and Colonel Harry Amory, and on it inscribed " in memory of many a good morning's harbouring and many a good day's hunting, 1896–1915."

The rapidity with which the deer thus increased proved the wisdom of Earl Fortescue's policy of keeping them within bounds, when as Lord Ebrington he was Master of the " Devon and Somerset " from 1881–1887. On killing a hundred deer in his first season there was an outcry that deer would be exterminated. This idea was altogether dispelled in the next few years when stronger measures in the shape of more hunting days and the formation of new packs had to be resorted to in order to keep the herds down.

Though not so numerous as formerly the numbers to-day are still great. This is largely due to the popularity of hunting with the farmers and other landowners who, recognising the sport stag-hunting gives and the welfare it brings to all the countryside, preserve deer in spite of the damage to crops that ensues.

Near shaves: Mist and rain in harbouring: A late harbour: A snapping twig and its result: A stag lies close to a road: A wet day and a timely find: A "best" mackintosh: A harbour on the Quantocks: A Dunster Meet: A providential find: A good end.

To be able to count the time in minutes before a meet is due and yet to have no idea of the whereabouts of a warrantable stag, is one of the most unenviable positions in which a harbourer can find himself. To be obliged to appear empty handed before the Master and an expectant Field is occasionally inevitable, but happily for my peace of mind providence in the shape of luck or experience—call it what you will—had a pleasant way of generally intervening to prevent it.

The worst enemies the harbourer has to contend with are mist and heavy rain. In the early autumn mornings it is common for a thick haze to hang over the moor until the sun is well up, by which time the deer have all settled down for the day. When this happens there is nothing to do but wait until the haze lifts, and then search the bracken to find antlers projecting above the ferns in which the deer are lying. A glimpse of these seen through powerful binoculars generally gives information sufficient to act upon, and in any case it is all one is likely to get.

Rain makes slotting difficult by filling the imprints with water, and so taking away that indescribable gloss that makes it possible to say when they have been freshly made.

One morning when I was harbouring on the moor for a meet at Brendon Two Gates the mist did not lift till half-past nine when it suddenly dissolved in bright sunshine. By that hour the deer had all gone to their resting-places, so I had to set about to see what I could find. A prolonged look round with the glasses failed to produce a sign of anything, and a ride through all the likely combes was equally disappointing. This, though annoying, was not altogether unexpected, for on account of three or four recent visits of the hounds to this district I knew most of the stags had gone to the coverts near Hawkcombe Head. A glance at my watch showed the hands were approaching within an uncomfortably close distance of eleven —the time of the meet. More minutes went by and I was still no nearer any result. At last it got so close on time that I could see through my glasses the horsemen gathering at Brendon Two Gates. Finally it wanted only five minutes to eleven, and I made up my mind we should have to go to the Hawkcombe Head coverts before we could hope to find anything. More or less giving it up as a bad job I turned my horse's head in the direction of Brendon Two Gates and started to ride towards the meet. On my way, at a spot called Three Combes Foot at the back of Larkbarrow, there were three largish clumps of ferns which I thought in passing just worth looking into. Fortunately, in spite of the lateness of the hour, I was not hurrying, and as I rode slowly upwind and alongside the nearest clump I had the intense satisfaction of catching sight of a pair of three-on-top horns. They were not more than thirty yards away and except for the tips of the antlers there was nothing else of the stag visible. Quickly turning my horse's head away I rode noiselessly off in the other direction. Almost immediately afterwards I fell in with a horseman on his way to the meet. By him I was able to send a message to the Master saying what had happened, while I adjourned to a neighbouring shepherd's cottage from where I should be able to observe the Field approaching and in the meantime be able to drink a cup of much-wanted tea. A few minutes later I rode out to meet the Field as it was streaming down from Brendon Two Gates and reported to the Master what I had seen. After a brief discussion as to the best line to take, it was decided I should put the stag up out of the fern and then, after a due amount of law had been given, the pack should be laid on. Thereupon, accompanied by Lord Ebrington who had expressed a wish to see the stag lying there, I rode off towards the clump of fern. In the meantime the Master arranged the field in such a fashion as to give the stag a chance to go over the forest. On coming to the edge of the clump I pointed out to Lord Ebrington just where I had seen the stag lying, and on this his lordship rode through the ferns until he considered he was close to the spot. So dense was this bracken patch that it was quite impenetrable to the eye for any distance, and Lord Ebrington finding himself unable to see any sign of the stag at the spot where it was supposed to be, proceeded, to my consternation, to stand upright on the saddle to get a wider view. What would have happened had the stag chosen that moment suddenly to spring up I do not know, for Lord Ebrington was riding a thoroughbred, and fine horseman as his lordship was, nothing could have stopped a nasty fall. Happily, the stag never stirred, and imploring Lord Ebrington to get back into the saddle I suggested a continuance of the search to put the stag up. With this his lordship rode all about the place where I thought the stag was lying, but came out of the fern again without having been able to find it. I then rode into the fern myself, and, feeling convinced the stag had not gone out, made a thorough search and in course of time put it up, thus illustrating again the desperation with which deer will cling to their belief in the safety of remaining unseen.

Another time when I was in a tight corner to find a stag, the situation was saved by the sound of a snapping twig. The meet was at Hawkridge and I was confidently relying on harbouring a stag in Whiterocks, the wood bordering the banks of the Barle close to where the Danesbrook flows into it, as has already been described. This wood is always a favourite place for stags, and for some days past several were known to have been feeding in a turnip field above the wood by night, and returning to lie in Whiterocks again by day. With the peculiar premonition for hunting days stags seem sometimes to possess, they had all on this particular morning gone off to find resting places elsewhere, and to add to my difficulties the day turned out foggy. I soon discovered slots that told me the deer had made off towards Anstey Common, but the fog was much too thick to allow any opportunity of seeing them. That being so, I considered the best chance of following up the deer lay in hitting off their slots again at the Five Cross Ways on the road to Anstey Burrows, for I thought it most likely they would be lying on the Common. Setting off to cast round Anstey Common I started to ride slowly along the road to Anstey Burrows. My eyes were fixed on the road in case there were any slots to be seen and my horse was jogging gently along, when a tiny twig suddenly snapped in the hedge that separated the road along which I was riding from the Common. Instantly turning my head but without making the slightest alteration in my horse's pace, I saw, projecting from the ditch on the other side of the hedge, the tips of a pair of antlers, each of which had three-on-top. Without making the slightest sign of having noticed anything I just continued quietly on at the same pace until I was well away out of sight and out of smell. The next thing was to wait until the fog lifted, which at last it did, and I thereupon rode down the road again to get to the meet. A number of people on their way to the same destination would, I knew, soon be passing along that same road, and this made it unlikely the stag would remain there until the hounds could arrive. He was, however, evidently well settled in, for when I passed him for the second time, the horns were visible exactly as they had been before. I thereupon hoped for the best, and after reporting to the Master, it was decided to draw the ditch with the pack. As soon as the hounds got to work, no fewer than three stags got up from the ditch, and that in spite of the proximity of the road and the number of people that must have ridden up and down it that morning. This harbouring incident may at first sight seem similar to that in which I harboured a stag in a hedgerow. It differs materially, however, in that the stags in this instance were lying under cover of a hedge that bordered a common on which they naturally like to lie. That they should choose a dry ditch nicely sheltered by a hedge on this common was, apart from the proximity to the road, nothing unusual, whereas in the other instance the chosen resting-place was an ordinary hedgerow simply separating two fields.

All these " last minute " harbourings represent hours of hard work beforehand which at times are very tiring. One day during the time Captain Adkins was Master, I left home about eight o'clock in the morning to find a stag for a meet at Winsford on the following day. Rain fell in torrents and after trying Red Cleeve, Allotments, Wick Wood, Burrow Wood, Punch Bowl, and the top part of the Barle Valley, all in drenching rain, I did not feel satisfied that I had anywhere seen the fresh slot of a good stag. I finished up by going to Withycombe Farm where Mr. Pring at once asked me to stay the night. I was out before daylight the next morning, and it was still raining as hard as ever. I began by looking to see if any deer had gone into the Punch Bowl or Ash Combe. Not finding anything, I again went over most of the ground I had tried the day before, including Burrow Wood, Allotments, Wick Wood and Red Cleeve, and again without seeing any signs of a warrantable stag.

Tired out and feeling thoroughly beaten to the world, I came out of Red Cleeve by Milton Rocks and started to ride up the Exe Valley road to Bridgetown, for it was now getting near the time for the meet. From the road I kept my eyes on the woods across the valley, and on coming opposite Hollam Wood I caught sight of something red showing up against a green patch. I immediately got my glasses on to it, and to my great relief saw it was a good huntable stag with two-on-top each side. It was now a quarter to eleven, and I set off to be at Winsford Hill at eleven with a light heart at finding a stag after such a long search in such terrible weather.

It was about this time that I struck the best mackintosh coat I ever had in my life. The weather had been rough for a long time and being fairly " fed up " with it, on meeting Tom Price in Dulverton one day I jokingly challenged .him to sell me a coat " to keep out the rain."

' I've got just the very thing," he replied. " You

shall have it on trial, and if it doesn't keep out the rain, I'll give it to you ! "

Nothing could be fairer than that, and taking it there and then I had an immediate opportunity of testing it over two of the wettest days it has ever been my lot to be out in. On the first day I harboured a stag at Haddon for Colonel H. H. Amory. After seeing this deer roused and the pack laid on in an unceasing fall of rain, I made straight off to Quantock Lodge a distance of some twenty miles or so in order to harbour a stag for the following day, for the " Devon and Somerset," then under the Mastership of Lord Bayford. The Quantock country was at that time being hunted by Mr. E. A. V. Stanley of Quantock Lodge, but this was the annual occasion on which by arrangement the " Devon and Somerset " hunted there. On arriving at Quantock Lodge I found Mr. Stanley was out with his own hounds, so thinking there might be some difficulty in finding a stag for the next day as hounds had just been through the woods, I went off to bed early in order to be up betimes in the morning. When I turned out before daybreak the rain was falling more heavily than ever, but clad in my precious mackintosh, which I was determined to test to the full before paying for it, I set off for Asholt Corner, which I knew would be a little sheltered. My luck was in that morning, for it was not long before I spotted something under a thorn bush on the opposite side of the valley that looked like a stag's horns. Holding my hat over my field-glasses to keep the wet off them, for it was still raining " cats and dogs," I saw a stag with three-on-top each side. Thankful to have got through the business so quickly I returned to Quantock Lodge to change into dry boots and socks. In spite of the heavy rain on two consecutive days the rest of my clothes were quite dry, so I had after all to pay for the coat. Whoever made it well earned his money! When the Master arrived with the hounds at eleven o'clock, the rain had at last ceased. The stag I had harboured in the morning was duly roused and killed at St. Audries. It was earmarked with a pig's ring, by which we knew it to be six years old.

It is bad enough to fail to find a stag on ordinary occasions, but what it feels like to face failure on extraordinary ones, when huge Fields and dense crowds of onlookers have come from far and near for a day's sport, I leave the reader to imagine. That was nevertheless within an ace of happening to me at a Dunster meet, one of the sporting events of the year that is held on the day after the Dunster Horse Show. The dry nature of the soil and the prevalence of gorse in the district makes slotting there difficult at any time, and on this occasion the greater part of two days' hard work had ended in nothing. I can tell you it was a tired man and a tired horse that had gone round nine coverts the day before; started the next morning at 4 a.m. to try all the woods between Slowley and Dunster; and now found themselves at 10.15 a.m. reined up on Frackford Bridge with no stag in hand. With no more likely woods left to explore and the meet due at eleven, the end seemed to have arrived. The situation was anything but pleasant, and rather than ride through the eager crowd of sightseers that would be thronging Dunster's ancient streets, and disappoint the Master by reporting a blank, I decided to take a gambler's chance to retrieve the day. Whatever happened now could not make things any worse. A message was therefore despatched to the Master at Dunster saying no deer had been harboured in the woods around, and asking if the hounds might be brought to Webbers Post. Towards this spot, over Dunkery, I made my way as fast as I could, though at that hour of the day I felt there was but little chance of finding a stag in time. When my horse and I got there, the long morning without food on the top of the arduous day before had begun to tell, and neither man nor beast was very far off the end of his tether. On reaching Boys Path, a spot from

(*Upper*) THE HARBOURER REPORTING TO THE MASTER
(*Lower*) A VIEW OF HADDON. THE TUFTERS OFF TO DRAW.

which I had in my time seen scores of stags, I dismounted and led my horse along it for about a hundred and fifty yards or so. At that point I stopped to look round, conscious this was about the last effort I could make. And then suddenly the unexpected happened. Over the opposite side of the valley on Cloutsham Ball a big stag leisurely rose out of the fern, shook himself, lazily looked round, and then settled down again out of sight. The sigh of relief I gave was a deep one, and the whole outlook of the day was changed. I looked at my watch and the time was exactly eleven. Hounds were at that moment meeting at Dunster. Rapidly calculating how long it would take them to reach Webbers Post after receiving my message, I decided to make the best use of my time by riding straight away to Cloutsham Farm, where through the generous hospitality of Major Vere Foster I obtained a feed for my horse and some breakfast for myself.

Happy and refreshed, we returned just in time to meet the hounds on their arrival at Webbers Post.

" Well, Fred, what have you got for us ? " was Colonel Wiggin's cheery greeting.

" A good stag lying over there, sir," was the reply, as I pointed out the thorn bush under which I had seen him lying. On that Colonel Wiggin decided to draw with the pack. Wending our way down along Priestway Path and thence on to the top of Cloutsham Ball, the hounds were held up while I rode into the fern and put the stag up. Up he jumped and away he went over Sweetery, and when time had been given for the Field to come up after him went the pack. A good run finally ended at Oare Ford, and so the day that began so unpromisingly finished successfully. If ever a horse and its rider were tired it was that night when they arrived home both as done to the world as man and beast can well be.

ON my appointment as head keeper to the Pixton Estate in 1904, I left Haddon to come down to Weir, where the keeper's house in Crewses's meadow lies only a few hundred yards from my present home. In spite of the extra work for the estate this new appointment entailed, it was the wish of the late Colonel the Honourable Aubrey Herbert that I should find the time to continue harbouring as before. To my other occupations that of pheasant rearing was now added. The labour necessary for this can be gathered from the fact that the shoots there were often big shoots that included a day of 960 head and many others when the numbers were round about 400 and 500 head.

Altogether I reared birds for about fifteen years to the total of somewhere about 35,000—the largest number for any one year being 6000.

A diary of the chief items of my work for the different months at this period comes out something like this :

April.—Harbouring for spring stag hunting.

May-July.—Pheasant rearing.

July (latter part) to 20th October.—Harbouring for stag-hunting.

October-1st February.—Organising shooting days ; harbouring hinds and rendering general assistance to the Hunt as required.

February-March.—Largely occupied in catching up stock pheasants for eggs for the coming season.

Add to these all the minor jobs inseparable from harbouring and keepering, and it will be gathered that the problem of what to do in my leisure time did not arise. When, through infirmities of age, Jim Wensley became no longer able to give me occasional help, I sometimes used to avail myself of assistance from Jim Gage. Gage has lived at Hartford all his life, and few men possess a better knowledge of slotting, a knowledge he also gained from the teaching of Old Jim.

To look after game is to become acquainted with many varieties of animals and birds, numbers of which are always on the look-out for an easy way of getting a living. Among the birds of prey, the sparrow hawk is incorrigible, and the kestrel, a useful feeder in other respects, succumbs to the temptation of tiny pheasants with regrettable ease.

The predatory instincts of these birds sometimes let them in for more than they bargain for.

One afternoon, some eighteen years ago, I was walking homewards across the fields between Allers* Wood and Pixton Park, when I saw a kestrel hovering in search of food. Suddenly it dropped in the usual stone-like manner, and picking up something in its talons, flew off. It had not flown far when suddenly changing its tactics the bird began rapidly to soar. Round and round in circles it flew higher and higher until it looked little larger than a starling. Then all of a moment its wings collapsed, and the hawk came hurtling down to earth just as if it had been shot. It fell with a thud only a few yards from where I was standing, and the moment it touched the ground a weasel escaped from its claws, and, apparently unhurt, ran down a hole in the earth close by. On examining the hawk I found the weasel had put its teeth right through the bird's neck, and brought about the almost instantaneous death I had just witnessed. A similar incident of a kestrel carrying off a weasel is recorded in Morris's *British Birds*, where it states that the kestrel " had not proceeded far when it was observed to fall from a considerable height. The weasel ran off unhurt, but the kestrel was found to have been killed by a bite in the throat."

The largest representative of the hawks in the

* Also known as Ellars.

West Country is the buzzard. Fortunately this bird has not fulfilled the predictions of older writers that it was becoming extinct, and in many districts it can now be seen in good numbers. Buzzards feed largely on young rabbits, mice, beetles and such-like, and though now and then one turns to young pheasants it is exceptional, and there is, generally speaking, no cause for the game preserver to molest them. The most curious episode I have seen a buzzard take part in was while crossing Anstey and Molland Commons early one morning on my way to Cuzzicombe Post. My horse was jogging gently along when I became aware of a buzzard flying slowly in front of me. The bird was about forty yards above the ground and about a hundred and fifty yards or so ahead of me, and for some little time this distance between us kept about the same. As I passed through the gate on to Molland Common and then turned to take a short cut along a by-path, the bird was still in front of me, and continued its flight slowly until it came over a patch of fern which, in the month of April, was still dead. Hovering over this brown patch for a few seconds like a kestrel, the bird then proceeded to pitch down on to the dead fern. From the saddle I could see it " beaking " at something, but as the back of the bird was towards me I could not see what it had got. At about thirty yards' distance the buzzard looked round, and, seeing me getting close, it flew off with some object in its claws. Rather to my surprise, it went back in almost exactly the same line it had come and in taking that direction it flew right over me. I looked up and instantly involuntarily shrank back, for the bird had a wriggling snake in its talons which looked as if it might at any moment fall. The buzzard, however, had no intention of any such thing happening, and with the squirming reptile safely clutched behind the head, went on its way. Buzzards are chronicled in books on natural history as sometimes eating snakes, and the snake in this instance, which I was able to see plainly as it was carried past me, I believe to have been a viper.

Vipers are very plentiful all over the Exmoor district. The warm spring sun soon wakes them up, and I have killed them when they have been lying out on a sunny bank in March while there was still snow on the ground. Their bite is dangerous to animals, and I have lost both dogs and sheep through them. Horses also have been known to be killed in this way. I remember a woman living on Haddon being very ill after a viper bite, but she got all right again, and I have never known anyone to die from this cause. Grass snakes and slow worms are found in numbers almost every-where, and no doubt account for many insects on which they largely feed. One fine evening in early summer when I was looking round a field of young pheasants, I heard a peculiar sound that somewhat resembled the noise a wounded hare sometimes makes, only not so loud. Remarking to the keeper with me that I thought there was a stoat about, I took my gun and cautiously stalked down the hedgerow in the direction of the sound. As I got close to the spot from where the sound was coming I saw the grass moving. Approaching gingerly to get a good shot at the stoat or weasel I supposed I should see, I was all the more aston-ished to come upon a large grass snake in the midst of attempting to swallow a toad. About half the body of the wretched toad was inside the snake's jaws but its head was still outside, and, while the struggling victim was making its peculiar cry of fear, the snake was exerting every effort to gulp it further down.

My sympathies were on the side of the vanishing toad, and stepping back I raised my gun and blew the body of the snake to pieces. I then proceeded to release the toad, which was quite a large one, with a stick. Thereupon it dragged itself off and disappeared in the grass apparently little the worse for its unpleasant adventure.

Badgers, though less plentiful than in former times, can still be found by those who know where to look for them. They cover a wide range in food, and though not usually troublesome they here and there call for proceedings against them. In one season pheasant's eggs kept unaccountably disappearing from Bury Castle—an ancient wooded earthwork close to Weir. For some time the cause of their disappearance was a mystery, until one day while examining one of the nests I found outside it some bits of eggshell looking as if something had been chewing them. I first of all suspected a fox had been there, but after carefully searching the wood a recently used badger's earth came to light. After more observations I came to the conclusion the badger was the culprit, and in due course he was dug out and killed. On opening the stomach the presence of eggshell proved my conclusions to be correct, and after that no more eggs disappeared.

The badger's power of excavating is well known. I once tried to keep a full-grown one, and put it into a walled enclosure with a solid lime and sand floor. For a few days all went well, and then one morning the badger was gone. Somehow or another it had dug right through the floor, and once down to earth the rest of course was easy. I remembered afterwards there was one little crack in the floor, and it must have been at that spot the badger first got a grip. Otherwise I don't think he could possibly have got through.

In 1907, about three years after I had been at Weir, Lord Bayford resigned the Mastership. How highly I value the handsome teapot and the photograph taken from the painting presented to his lordship by the Hunt, which Lord Bayford presented me with on his retirement, I need scarcely say. They are lasting mementoes of twelve very happy years of my life.

Lord Bayford was followed by Mr. E. A. V. Stanley who, after holding office for two years, was succeeded by Captain (now Major) Adkins.

From hunting the Quantocks, Mr. Stanley not only came to the " Devon and Somerset " with a long experience of stag-hunting, but also augmented the pack with hounds he brought with him. He used to hunt the hounds himself alternately with his huntsman, and, with the wonderfully fleet horses he kept, accounted for a large number of deer. Mr. Stanley was one of the hardest riders to hounds I ever met. As a Master he could be severe when occasion required and we have many times laughed at the way he would rap some of the erring hunting visitors over the knuckles. I well recollect a day when, after a good run from the forest, hounds had brought their stag to the water in the Horner Valley under Cloutsham, some of the more eager of the Field were overriding them. Casting his hounds to try to hit off the line they had lost when the stag went to water Mr. Stanley put up with the annoyance for some time. At last being unable to stand it any longer he reined in his horse, and turning round in the saddle to face the delinquents shouted sarcastically, " I should think all you ——s have got a half-holiday to-day."

An interesting feature of the Exe and Haddeo Valleys are the herons which the Pixton heronry supplies. This heronry which is now in Allers* Wood just beyond the borders of Pixton Park, is known to have existed before 1545†. In those days the birds built in Shelveacre Wood near Combe. Disturbed by timber cutting they moved at one time to Steart Wood inside the park, and for a similar reason they later on went from there to Allers Wood, where they still remain.

Their numbers usually keep fairly constant and average about nine to a dozen nests or so a year, but have been rather fewer this year. Next door to the heronry in another part of the same wood there is a large rookery, but the two do not appear to interfere with each other at all.

---

* Also known as Ellars.
† See "The Heron in Somerset," by B. W. Tucker. (*Proceedings of the Somerset Archæological Natural History Society*, Vol. LXXV, 1929.)

I suppose the two rarest natural history specimens I have come across in this part of the country have been a roebuck and a golden eagle. The roebuck I shot in Pezzlecombe Wood close to Weir and its head is at Pixton. How it came to be in Pezzlecombe Wood I have not the least idea, as I have never heard of any being nearer than Dorset.

The golden eagle I also saw in Pezzlecombe Wood. It was perched on a tree, and my attention was first drawn to it by the glint of the sun on its back, and also by the great size of the bird. By stalking carefully up behind the trees I was able to get quite a near view of it. After a time it leisurely spread its wings and flew off up the Morebath Valley. A few days later I saw in the paper a golden eagle had been shot in Dorset. I presumed this was the same bird, but of its actual history I have no knowledge.

CHAPTER XI   NATURE OF WILD RED DEER

WILD red deer take their title from the tawny colour of their coats. The colour of hinds differs little if at all from that of stags, but on the whole the stag is perhaps rather more red.

The colour shows but few variations except during the rutting season, when the hair round the necks of stags becomes darker and owing to the swelling of the neck looks shaggier and longer. Piebald deer have I believe been recorded, but I have never myself known a wild red deer in the West Country to have any white patches. Where any appearance suggesting this has been observed, it has on closer examination usually turned out to be the result of loss of hair that has been knocked off in jumping or some other accidental way.

The majority of hinds drop their calves from the second to the third week in June. Opinions differ as to the precise dates on which most of the young deer are born, and the occurrence of a certain number of variations is of course only to be expected.

Dr. Palk Collyns stated he knew of " but two

instances in which the hind did not drop her calf between the 7th and the 21st of June."* He disagrees with the writer of the *Art of Venerie*, whom he quotes as saying "that when a hinde would conceive, she attendeth untill the star Arcture be raysed, and caryeth her calfe eight or nine months, the which are calved in May commonly, altho' I have seen some fall later, according to the nouriture and age of the hinde."

For myself I have never known a wild red deer in the West Country calve before the 15th June, though I know of others who say they have.

Occasionally I have known them calve as late as the beginning of July and one or two even as far on as September, but in the great majority the event occurs round about the 24th of June. It is surprising how soon newly born calves begin to get on their legs. They can sometimes be seen standing or making little efforts to follow the mother about within two or three hours of being dropped.

The nursery routine is at first strict. In the morning after the mother has duly given her offspring its breakfast and proudly watched it playing around for a time, she tells it, in the language of deer, to go to bed. Thereupon the little fellow obediently runs off and lies down

* *Chase of the Wild Red Deer.*

134

under a fairly adjacent bush, say some forty or fifty yards away. There he remains until the hind comes to him again. Should any danger threaten, the calf signals its alarm by a bleat that somewhat resembles the sound made by a hare. On hearing this the hind immediately flies to her offspring's assistance. Should the intruder be one she can hope to deal with, as for instance a dog of no great size, the hind will often show fight by striking out angrily with her forefeet, or otherwise she will try to practise some sort of self-sacrifice by attracting the enemy's attentions to herself and so drawing off the danger from her calf. At birth the calf is spotted, and remains so until about the end of September, when the winter coat of the same colour as other deer is assumed. This dappling makes the calves very inconspicuous amongst the lights and shades of summer foliage. It thus gives them additional protection for the first few months, during which they are difficult to see, and only the trained eye can at that period hope to distinguish them. Hinds mate with stags after attaining their second year of age, *i.e.* in the October following their birth in the June of two years before. After their first calf they usually give birth to another every year until their age for reproduction is over. A few lose their calves either before or after birth, but the great majority bring their young successfully to maturity. The question of twins is of interest. In the opinion of some people twins do not occur at all, but with that view I do not agree. Dr. Palk Collyns* discusses the question at some length. He quotes from the *Art of Venerie* to the effect that " there are some hinds which have two calves at once," and gives in addition three instances in which the evidence appeared to him to be conclusive of this event.

One was an observation made on 16th of June 1790 by the Sir T. D. Acland of that time, regarding a hind in Birchwood with two calves, apparently about two days old. The second instance arose from the general testimony of accredited persons in 1858 concerning a hind in the Horner coverts that was known to have twins running by her side. The third case was based on evidence of an experienced forester who stated that he knew of a hind that had produced twins, both males ; that he had seen them fed by the mother on the day of their birth, and subsequently watched them grow to maturity.

My own opinion is that hinds certainly bear twins occasionally, though the occurrence is not more frequent than the bearing of twins by mares. The first case I ever knew of was in Storridge, where

* *Chase of the Wild Red Deer.*

136

two calves not more than a couple of days old were running about with the hind. I have also seen what I believe to have been undoubtedly twin calves with their mothers on several occasions at Cloutsham and on other parts of the forest. It may be taken as a general rule that no two stags are quite alike. Practically living among them and watching them growing up from year to year as I used to do, I got to recognise them individually like a shepherd knows his sheep.

The only exception to this rule that I can remember occurred in two stags that used to frequent Badgworthy Common at the top of the Doone Valley. They were always to be seen together, and were so exactly alike that I could see no distinguishing points of difference anywhere. Each had brow and tray points with two-on-top each side, and in length also their antlers were about the same, not being more than about fifteen inches long in either of them. So struck was I with the close resemblance they bore to each other that I asked the late Mr. Nicholas Snow of Oare, always a true friend to the hunting fraternity, to come to look at them with me. He, too, saw the likeness, and agreed they were probably twins as I always believe them to have been. One morning during the spring stag-hunting season when three and four-year-olds are hunted, I harboured these two and one of them was killed. From that day onwards I never saw the other one again. Losing its companion and driven from its usual haunts, it doubtless joined another herd further off.*

By the time August stag-hunting comes in, the calves have acquired considerable activity and staying powers. Should they be disturbed when hounds are after a stag, hind and calf run together for a little way until, seeing a suitable hiding place, the hind orders the calf off into a bush while she endeavours to draw off the danger by running in the opposite direction. So skilful is the hind in thus manœuvring that only very seldom indeed is a calf ever accidentally killed by hounds. After the disturbance in a wood is over, whether it has been caused by stag-hounds, fox-hounds or sheep-dogs, any of which may stir up the deer, and everything is all quiet again, the hinds return to find their calves. I have waited to see them come back in Sweetery, Haddon and other places, and have watched the reunion with great interest. While still some distance from the wood the hinds trot along or walk fast. As they get nearer they become more careful, frequently looking round and sniffing the air for any suspicious signs. At last,

* A similar instance in which two stags, believed to have been twins, and always seen in each other's company, is quoted by Dr. Palk Collyns.

satisfied that all is well, they give a call, the sound of which is difficult to convey in words, but it is something like a shrill " baa " of a sheep. This is answered by a plaintive cry from the wood, and in a few moments the calf comes running out to join its mother. Great is its joy at seeing her back again, and after a little playfulness it loses no time in getting some milk. When the meal is over the mother watches her offspring at play, and, should there be two or three calves in the neighbourhood they jump about together and frolic like lambs, while the old hinds stand by proudly looking on.

Apart from accidental death, which on account of the cleverness of the hinds is not at all frequent, the mortality of calves is slight and the herds rapidly increase in size. I once saw the carcase of a tiny calf lying on a large ant heap in Horner Wood. The ants had reduced it to a skeleton, but whether the little fellow had happened to drop by the side of the ant heap to die or whether he had lain there by chance and been overwhelmed by the insects I cannot say.

The rutting season for Exmoor deer commences about the second week of October. In the Porlock district down by the sea where the temperature is in the main higher and the " keep " better, I have known it to begin a little sooner. The season lasts throughout the month and as mentioned earlier in the chapter, hinds first mate with stags in the autumn following their second birthday.

With the onset of rutting the appearance and character of stags abruptly alter. The hair on their necks becomes darker, and the neck itself swells. From being timid they become fierce and defiant, no longer congregating in herds; they wander off separately each with a chosen band of hinds. At this time they readily fight with each other, and in some circumstances become dangerous to man. This is the season too in which stags are to be heard " belling " — a long drawn-out dismal roar which often ends in a series of fierce barks or grunts. " Belling " goes on by day and night, and heard at close quarters for the first time when all else is still, it can be very frightening. In narrating his first experience of this weird sound heard for the first time above the growl of thunder while riding along Hartford Bottom during a storm, Dr. Palk Collyns likens it to a sound seeming to proceed from the bowels of the earth and one so passing strange that he had never heard the like before, and it was not—he tells us—until he had galloped some half a mile from the spot that he felt his pulse beating as usual.

" Belling " is a command to the hinds in the neighbourhood to gather round, and on hearing it those not already attached flock to join the stag that is calling them. The fierce barks or grunts often heard at the end of the " belling " are of belligerent character and serve as a challenge to other stags around to clear out or fight. I have never known a stag under four years old to bellow, though they sometimes make a noise somewhat like that of a calf. Only the bigger ones roar really loudly, and whenever typical " belling " is heard a warrantable stag may be surmised to be behind it. Among themselves stags fight freely and fiercely, and I shall always remember an encounter I once had the good fortune to witness. The scene was laid on Haddon Hill and the time was a peaceful Sunday evening. I had been taking a walk and was wandering leisurely over the hillside towards home when I heard two stags suddenly begin to roar at each other. One was in Hurscombe Wood and the other in Deer Park Wood. From the fierceness of the barks and grunts that followed the roaring there was no doubt they meant business, so thinking to see something interesting I squatted down among the heather and waited. After more challenging from both sides, two large stags emerged one from each wood, and bellowing loudly all the time, they advanced towards each other in the open. My position happened to be somewhere about midway between the two woods, so that when the stags got within sparring distance of each other the field of battle was not more than from fifty to a hundred yards away. As the stags approached each other boldness gave way to wariness, and when about thirty yards distant from one another they began to manœuvre for position. Gradually getting nearer and nearer and roaring loudly all the time, the two deer sidled round and round, each with his head sideways inclined to seek an opening to the other's ribs. At last one of them got in a strong thrust, but with " foot work " of a rapidity that would have done credit to a champion boxer, his antagonist's head was round in time to parry the blow with safety. For a while they wrestled with antlers interlocked, and then breaking away they skirmished for position as before. With tongues out and the hair on their backs standing up with anger, they fought on, frothing, sweating and grunting. Now they were butting with antlers interlocked, now they were on their knees, and now breaking free, they were working round each other again to fence for a knock-out blow. With all the strength and fighting skill at their command they battled on, and for a whole hour and twenty minutes fought unceasingly without advantage to either. So evenly matched were they that sheer exhaustion seemed the only likely solution. Then came an unexpected and dramatic end. A fierce belling getting nearer and nearer heralded the approach of a third stag. Hurrying to the scene of the fray he passed near enough to give me an uncomfortable feeling lest the pair should decide to leave their domestic differences unsettled and attack their common foe. Nothing, however, happened, and the newcomer without deigning to take the slightest notice of me walked on towards the fighting pair. Within a few yards of them he stopped dead, and for a few seconds stood perfectly still and contemplated them. Then all of a moment, without any warning whatever, he lowered his head and charged one of the antagonists fiercely in the flank. This altogether unexpected and unfair blow separated the antagonists, and sent the victim of it reeling for several feet down the side of the hill. Regaining his footing and recovering from his surprise he stood looking at his original enemy. For a few seconds the two glared at each other. Then apparently content that honour had been sufficiently satisfied, or what is much more likely, terrified by the possibilities of what they might get from the new arrival, they turned and each went his own way. The third stag, now complete master of the situation, stood, belling with triumph, looking at them. At this point I got up and showed myself, and the last comer then also trotted off.

In the whole of my experience no deer has ever offered to attack me or " drive me up a tree," as related in legendary tales of farmers returning home late from fairs. My experience is that so long as wild deer are in the open they will, as soon as they realise they are up against a human being, run away. In the difficulties of harbouring them I have indeed often wished they would be a little bolder. It is, however, quite possible if their way along some narrow path were obstructed they might charge, and after the velvet is off their horns they will fight fiercely when at bay.

When deer are confined in parks or other enclosures it is another matter, and their possible danger in such circumstances during the rutting season is well known. At such times it is always well to be on the safe side and give them a wide berth.

What on one occasion appeared to have the possibilities of a serious tragedy turned the next moment into an amusing comedy. A stag that was getting beat towards the end of a run was making for the river at Exebridge. In his efforts to dodge the hounds he took to doubling backwards and forwards within a fairly small area. These backward and forward journeys kept taking him to and fro under a railway bridge, and by this time the prospect of a kill in the near future had attracted a goodly number of local sightseers. Among the most enthusiastic of them was an elderly farm labourer who with trousers tied up below the knees and elbows bent in the orthodox position of eager runners, capered towards the bridge which the stag had shortly before passed through. Unfortunately for him the stag had changed its tactics and unexpectedly turned back, thereby bringing man and deer face to face as each was entering the arch. Hastily the old man turned to fly, but the breath he had so freely spent in the pursuit was exhausted and he was not quick enough. The stag lowered its antlers to charge, and the Field held its breath. For a moment we all thought the old man's end had come, and then a roar of laughter suddenly went up when it was realised the stag had done nothing worse than take out the seat of the old man's corduroy trousers, a roar which redoubled in intensity as the victim was seen sheepishly backing towards the nearest hedge for shelter. Half a crown from Major Greig, the Master, quickly restored the old man's equanimity, and the chase then went on.

CHAPTER XII   HABITS OF WILD RED DEER

ANYONE who is disposed to regard deer as harmless animals should take a look at a turnip field on which they have recently been feeding. It is not so much the quantity of food they devour as the amount they lay waste in obtaining it.

Stags, like all other animals, prefer to get their food with the least possible trouble to themselves. When they have taken one or possibly two bites at a turnip and thereby pulled it out of the ground so that it rolls about, they no longer bother about it but pass on to the next one, which they proceed to treat in a similar way. It does not require much imagination to understand how deer by feeding in this wasteful manner can ruin a good part of a field of turnips in a night. The idea which has found its way into books that stags take one bite at a turnip and then wantonly throw it over their shoulder while hinds eat them less wastefully is not altogether in accordance with facts. In all the scores of times I have watched stags feeding I have never seen them act deliberately in that manner. What they do is to bite at the

146

same turnip only so long as it remains in the ground, and thereby giving them something fixed to pull at. Once the turnip is pulled out of the ground, as usually happens after the first or second bite, it naturally rolls about and becomes troublesome to control. That does not suit the stag, so he just leaves it and passes on to the next. The amount devoured from each turnip depends therefore on its fixity in the soil, which varies under different conditions of seasons and weather, and is not necessarily limited to only one capricious bite. Hinds are perhaps inclined to give rather more attention to individual turnips than stags, but I do not consider the appearance of the turnips alone affords sufficient evidence as to whether a stag or a hind has been eating them.

Amongst corn, deer are equally destructive. They will trample all over a field taking mouthfuls only here and there, and crushing the corn still more by lying down in it whenever they feel inclined. They eat off the ears and leave the straw, so that when they have finished the field looks like a bed of rushes. Young shoots of the ash rank high in their estimation, and when these are plentiful deer will sometimes remain in the woods for days on end. The effect on a young ash covert after a feast of this kind can be well imagined. Deer are very fond of the berries of mountain

147

ash, and it is most amusing to see what antics both stags and hinds will practise in order to obtain them. To begin with they walk sedately round the trees picking off everything within reach. Next they get up on their hind legs and pick off any branches they can seize in that way, and when that method no longer gives fruitful results I have seen old stags standing up on their hind legs and rattling the trees with their antlers to bring the berries down. Hinds endeavour to do the same but possessing no horns they have frequently to forego much of what the stag manages to reach.

Apples, with a strong preference for sweet varieties, are always an attraction, and since deer treat orchards in a somewhat similar way to which they treat a turnip field, their visits are looked upon by the farmer as being anything but popular.

Their greed for apples often ends in their thoroughly gorging themselves, and stags harboured after recently feeding in orchards seldom run very far. I have once seen a stag eating blackberries which seemed to give considerable pleasure. The best diet for keeping deer both fit and fat is plenty of acorns. Deer are very fond of them, and a good acorn year, by keeping the deer in the woods, often proves of great advantage to the deer-

148

damage fund, out of which compensation is paid for injury to crops.

When stags elect to remain in the woods for days on end, harbouring them often becomes difficult. It sometimes necessitates searching inside the wood, and, in dry weather, slots on the paths and rides are anything but easy to find. It is seldom a stag has satisfied his hunger sufficiently to make him spend a night resting on the moor, but I have met with one instance in which this appeared to be so. Hounds were meeting at Yard Down and I was staying with the late Mr. Robins of Lydcot Hall in the Bray Valley with the idea of harbouring a stag thereabouts for the following day. Yard Down is always a popular meet on account of the likelihood of a good run over the forest, so I was all the more annoyed at not being able to find signs of any huntable stags. In spite of Mr. Robins wishing me to stay the night as had been arranged, there was no getting over the necessity of looking elsewhere. With that in view, I set off after tea intending to go on to Simonsbath and harbour a stag on the forest there. On my way over Whitefield Down, soon after leaving Lydcot, I, however, saw what proved on looking through my glasses to be the tops of a stag's horns showing under a thorn bush. They had three-on-top each side, but beyond that I could not see any other details. This lucky find solved my difficulties, and back I went to Lydcot where Mr. Robins gave me a warm welcome, and all the more so because it meant hounds coming there the next day. Before daybreak on the following morning, accompanied by Mr. Robins, I was at the bottom of Whitefield Down waiting for it to get light enough to see something of my friend of the evening before if possible. I expected either to catch sight of him on the moor as he came in from feeding or to slot him down the valley into the woods, if that should be the line he chose to go. Not seeing anything moving on the moor, I directed my glasses on to the thorn bush again as soon as the light was good enough to distinguish details, and to my delight the pair of three-on-tops were exactly in the position they had been the day before. So still were they that Mr. Robins laughingly suggested the stag might be dead. However, after we had waited patiently for some time a bright ray from the rising sun fell on the bush and we could see the head move. This at any rate proved the stag was very much alive, and we returned to Lydcot for breakfast. When the time came for the tufting, every effort was made to direct the stag on to the open moor, but he decided otherwise and was killed at Hole Water. He was a very fat stag, and was doubtless taking a comfortable rest after a good gorge a day or two previously on some luckless farmer's crops.

Deer swim very well and are fond of the water. When they take to it they are said to " soil." They make a special practice of this in the rutting season, choosing for the purpose any pond or peat pit they happen to meet with. The more muddy it is, the more they seem to relish it, and rolling over and over they wallow in mud and slime until they have made themselves into a proper mess. When they have finished they stand up and shake themselves. While being hunted deer often go to the water to refresh themselves and also at times to hide. For the latter purpose they generally choose a spot where the stream is overhung with bushes and where the banks are high. They will then get out of sight and squat in the water with only their noses above the top to enable them to breathe. Time after time I have known deer to escape in this way.

Dr. Palk Collyns tells of the fright a fisherman once got by accidentally stirring up a stag that had successfully evaded the hounds in this manner. On going to fish during the evening a net the man was using became entangled in the hind leg of the deer, with the result that both the net and the fisherman were dragged across the river. So upset was the frightened man that he at once made for home and sought Dr. Collyn's professional services. After telling the cause of his fright the man added with a fearful sigh, " It was the devil, zur ; I do know it, I seed his *cloven foot.*" In vain Dr. Collyns tried to persuade him of his error, and not until he took the man to the spot the next morning and there showed him the slots of the deer where it had left the river could he convince him of his mistake.

When a stag has taken to the water and gone up or down stream according to his fancy, the sagacity of hounds in dealing with the situation is particularly instructive to watch. There being no scent from the water to guide them, and realising as well as we do or perhaps better the nature of the problem to be solved, the hounds divide their forces. Some going on one side of the river and some on the other, they cast up or down the stream according to the direction they think the stag has taken. Bushes overhanging the water which the stag may have inadvertently touched are all sniffed. Should a hound scent the deer from one of them he at once gives tongue and all the others dash up to him to help in taking up the line. On coming to barring poles that are put across the stream to divide fields and prevent cattle from straying down the water, hounds with equal eagerness sniff the woodwork for a sign of the deer having passed, while to the huntsman, recent splashes on the bars that have not yet had time to dry often tell a useful tale.

On the general question of scent, why it is good some days and poor on others there are many theories to which I have nothing of value to add. Speaking generally my own opinion is that scent is best when the weather is settled either fine or wet. I remember one season at the time Major Greig was Master, when in spite of drought and heat, and dust everywhere flying up from the heather, Sidney Tucker killed something like seventeen or eighteen stags in succession. I have known days when hounds could follow the scent of hinds more easily than that of stags, but I can offer no explanation of the reason.*

Allusion has frequently been made to the craftiness deer show in endeavouring to evade hounds. In tufting it is always the young stags and hinds that leave the coverts first, while the old stags lie close hoping to the end they will remain unseen. When being hunted, old stags search systematically for young ones to take their place. They habitually make for coverts where other deer are known to be, and having found them they will deliberately put up any young stag they

* The French hold that the scent of rutting stags is distasteful to hounds and that their scent differs after they have lost their horns.

153

find lying there with the idea of providing a substitute for the hounds to follow. It is commonly stated that having put up a younger stag from its bed, the older one that is being hunted lies down in the vacated place. Such a procedure would clearly be useless, for the hounds, hard on the trail, would naturally come right on to the deer they were hunting at the spot where he has stopped to lie down in the younger one's bed before they could pick up the line of the fresh one that has just got up. The hunted stag would thus simply be waiting, so to speak, for hounds to come up to him. What does happen, and what I have actually seen, is that on putting a younger stag up, the older one that is being hunted sides away into the thicket off the line. The result of this manœuvre is that hounds following the original stag suddenly come on a direct line of hot scent at the spot where the fresh one has got up. This scent they eagerly follow, while their first stag makes his way off quietly on his own. These are occasions on which the huntsman can frequently turn his skill to good account by recognising the loud change of note hounds often make on picking up a fresh hot scent. To the experienced huntsman a change of note of this kind denotes hounds have either gone over to a fresh deer or worked up to their first stag and " fresh found " him. When, perhaps a mile or two further on, the huntsman finds himself able to verify his suspicions of a fresh deer, he stops his hounds and, to the surprise of the Field, who for the most part have not realised what has happened, brings them all the way back to the spot where they changed their cry. From there they often-times again pick up the trail of the original stag, which instead of making good use of his time to get right away has been hanging about on the strength of his believed escape.

From time to time rumours arise of *girt* black stags haunting the forest. Every year these big stags are credited with escaping the notice of harbourer and huntsman in some miraculous way until finally they rise in the imagination of the countryside to be the " biggest girt stag ever seen." When their time comes, as one day it surely does, they turn out to be big old stags that have certainly up to then cleverly managed to evade the hounds. In colour they are darker than usual, a variation that is due to staining of their coats by the murky moorland peat water in which they continually " soil." Even so, the tint is only a little deeper than normal, but seen with a keen imagination on a misty morning it easily assumes an exaggerated hue. Apart from their slightly darker colour such stags do not differ

155

otherwise in any way from their younger companions. One of the kind long known as the " Black Stag of Badgworthy " is recorded by Mr. Philip Everard as giving hounds their last run of the season in 1893.

A question sometimes raised is how it happens that some well-known old stags are seen only quite at the end of the hunting season or after hind-hunting has begun. The reason they are more likely to be seen at the end of the season is probably due to their coming more into the open for the rutting time, the first week or so of which tends somewhat to overlap the last two weeks of stag-hunting.

Why they frequently escape notice earlier in the season is, I think, capable of more than one explanation. On the Hawkcombe Head side of the moor, for instance, many old stags in my opinion make their homes down in the cliffs where the sea breezes probably aid in keeping flies away, and where the hounds seldom go to find them. In other places like Haddon and Hawkridge many lie in out-of-the-way gorse brakes and coverts, which are not unlikely to escape attention. On account of the number of good stags nearer at hand the harbourer has usually no reason to search these more out-of-the-way places for the three meets or so which, as a rule, are all that are held each season in these districts. These deer are therefore often never harboured, a fact that is the more understandable when one remembers that the harbourer's policy is mainly :

(1) To harbour a stag as near as possible to the meet : (2) to select one which will cause as little delay as possible in tufting : and (3) to select one that seems likely from its position to go away towards open country and give a good run.

Given these general rules, my ambition was always to pick out the biggest stag with the best head I could find, and being satisfied with that there must, considering the number of stags about, still be many not accounted for.

As an illustration of an unlikely place for a big stag to lie and one which but for accident would doubtless have been overlooked, I can recall a day when I was harbouring for a meet at Cloutsham. As usual I arrived on the afternoon of the day before the meet, and the late Mr. Partridge of Horner Farm came to have a chat about hunting, as he often did when I was that way. This time he was worried about a stag that had been eating turnips in one of his fields below the road leading from Luckham to Horner. " I would be glad if you would harbour him in the morning, because he is doing a lot of damage," he said. I replied that I would do my best.

Instead, however, of going to see what slots the turnip field showed, I took up my usual stand before daybreak on Boys Path on Dunkery. From there I saw three stags, two of which were good ones, come in over by the " wind and weather " hut on Horner Hill, and proceed to lie down in the woods below. " These," I said to myself, " are no doubt the deer that have been troubling Mr. Partridge," and on that conclusion I thought it would be of little use to go to the turnip field. I had, however, promised I would go, so I went on just to say I had been. In the field, sure enough, there were slots of an old stag that had been eating the roots that morning. My next move was to try the road leading from Luckham to Horner to see which way he had gone. To my surprise there was nothing to show he had ever crossed the road, and on this I at once realised the stag in question could not be one of the three I had seen earlier in the morning. I therefore re-entered the turnip field and took up the trail again. At the far end of the field there was a tiny little wood, looking barely half an acre in extent, called Copperclose Copse, and into that the slots undoubtedly led. A cast all round this copse gave no signs of outgoing slots, so the only conclusion I could arrive at was that the stag was lying there. On the tufters arriving the stag was out in half a minute, and after that day he troubled Mr. Partridge's turnip field no more.

A little covert of that kind seemed a most unlikely place for an old stag to lie in, but it is, I am sure, in such unlikely places that many old deer keep themselves tucked away until the approach of the rutting season, when they begin to move about more. There are many outside gorse brakes and all sorts of spinneys and other out-of-the-way places which unless systematically searched are safe hiding for months at a time. I knew of two stags last year that left Haddon in the stag-hunting season to make their home in the brakes of Woolcots Valley, a mile or two away. They were one morning put up by the fox-hounds while cubbing, but they escaped the attention of the stag-hounds throughout the season.

This habit of lying in what would appear to be the most unlikely spots is not infrequently the cause of the tufting failures.

One day when there was a meet at Heathpoult, and stags had been feeding on oats belonging to that good old sportsman, Mr. Robert Norman, I slotted them into Oaktrow Wood. Slotting there was a simple matter, because a cart track ran down through the wood and the main road lay at the bottom of it, and on both of these I should have easily seen slots had the deer crossed them to leave the wood after they had entered it.

After reporting the whereabouts of the stags to the Master, the pack was kennelled at Oaktrow Farm and the tufters were taken into the wood. After drawing first the most likely and then the less likely parts we still found no signs of the deer. The ground was just right that morning for easy slotting, so jumping off my horse, which a lady kindly undertook to hold for me, I entered the wood and picked up the slots I had previously tracked down at the place where the deer had gone in. They zig-zagged a good deal, but all the time kept leading in a downward direction. Finally I got almost to the bottom of the wood, and within about fifty yards of the main road, where by this time scores of horsemen were gathered. The undergrowth now became very thin, but still the slots went on though it was hard to see where the stags could be lying. Then out of the only patch of bracken of any size they suddenly got up. Unless I had been absolutely sure the stags were there I should not have thought that lower bit of wood with its proximity to the main road and scarcity of undergrowth worth troubling about.

A further cause for failure to find stags may lie in the fact that although the slots lead up to a wood, the stags may have never actually gone into it. One morning when harbouring on Bickingcott Farm before it was quite daylight I could just discern through my glasses two brown objects walking amongst yellow wheat. I watched them for a long time and as the light got better I saw them making for an ash fence as though to enter the wood. Not content with gorging on wheat they dallied along the fence and began to pick off ash shoots. Finally they turned sharply back and walked into the middle of the field where they proceeded to lie down. Had I not seen them it would have been easy to have concluded from the slots that they had gone into the wood, for with numerous inward and outward going slots all made within a few minutes of each other it would be impossible to say for certain which of all were the last made.

Many deer live to a comparatively old age, but my impression is that fewer of the old ones escape notice now than was formerly the case. This I attribute largely to the use of more powerful field-glasses. By their aid it is often possible to single out an old stag from characteristics it would with less efficient vision be difficult to discern. Then again an old deer is sometimes overlooked through possessing disproportionately small slots —a notable instance of which I have already related in the case of the stag with seventeen points. Earl Fortescue has drawn my recollection to a stag that was killed in the Exe under Staddon Hill during the time Colonel Hornby was Master. This stag was shrunken all over, and his slots were very small. From an ear mark it was thought to be one that had been taken at Hawkridge sixteen or seventeen years before. My own impression of stags that appear shrunken is that they have probably always been what I call "little-old-stags" or, as the local farmers would say, a little "nestle tripe," meaning thereby the little odd one of the family.

When I am asked how long deer naturally live I am obliged to say with many others that I do not know. It is exceedingly rare to find a dead stag, though presumably one here and there might be expected to die from old age. In most of the dead ones I have come across the cause of death has generally been fairly clear. Four or five I have known to be gored to death by their fellows in the rutting season. A few appeared to have died from some internal disease, and in others accident has been the cause.

Of these latter there was the stag I have already mentioned that died through getting his antlers entangled in the root of a tree. Occasionally also deer get their hind legs hung up between the

(*Upper*) MEET AT CLOUTSHAM
(*Lower*) HELE BRIDGE. BRINGING OUT THE TUFTERS.

layers of fences, and are unable to free them-selves.

What, if any, is the value of evidence to show that deer sometimes live for a hundred years or more I cannot tell, but I can say that I have never seen or heard of anything to make me think it could apply to West Country deer. Were I to hazard a guess at the natural length of life of these, I should say those that are lucky enough to die 'from old age would be from seventeen to twenty years.

The mentality of West Country deer has many points of interest. Allusion has been made to the various ways in which they react to danger according to the times of year such as the rutting season, when they are fierce, and the early summer-time when, bereft of their horns, they hide away. Their natural methods of avoiding danger are by flight or by lying close according to the circum-stances to which each seems best suited. Their behaviour when anyone passes them is also variable. Sometimes they will gallop away in a great fright. At other times, whether standing up or lying down, they will cunningly follow the passer-by with their eyes without otherwise moving, provided they think they are unseen. The best way not to alarm them is to pass them by quite unconcernedly without appearing to pay the slightest attention to them. Any alteration in the pace, whether walking or riding, or stopping to look at them will almost surely send them off. This behaviour is in general accordance with that which they show when the tufters are about. That is, they are content to remain where they are so long as they imagine they have not been discovered.

Like most other animals their curiosity is easily aroused, and this is no doubt one of the factors that accounts for herds sometimes standing on a hill and gazing down on moving objects below.

There is a popular belief that stags know when the season for hunting them is over. Whether this is so or not it must be admitted they often behave as if they knew it.

After the rutting season is over stags begin to congregate together again ; and on such places as Haddon, Dunkery, Molland Common and Hawkridge, I have seen herds of as many as from fifteen to twenty coolly looking on while hounds were hunting hinds. Their chivalry on such occasions is non-existent. Not only do they offer no help by trying to draw off the hounds as they are so fond of forcing others to do for themselves, but they will actually butt and drive away any hunted hind that seeks to approach the herd for shelter. I have frequently seen this happen and I can only say that had the same stags seen hounds closely approaching them during the hunting season, they would not have waited long to look on.

However much one may try to lay down rules for the behaviour of deer one can never be the least sure what they will do when it comes to the point, and more often than not it is the unexpected that happens. Mention has for instance been made in different chapters of the way younger deer usually scurry away before the tufters, leaving their elders to stay behind until driven up. I remember, however, in one spring stag-hunting season, when three and four-year-olds are hunted, a young stag behaving with extraordinary coolness in the face of hounds. The meet was with Sir John Amory's stag-hounds at Cuzzicombe Post, and I had harboured a young stag in West Molland Wood. While tufting for him I was riding through a wood just in front of Mr. Ludovic Amory who was that day hunting hounds, when I suddenly saw the stag I had harboured lying just below us in an old charcoal pit. We stopped our horses to look at him and waited, expecting the tufters, which were close at hand, to put him up. Seeing he was observed and there being no under-growth in the pit to serve as any sort of conceal-ment, the stag got up but did not offer to move away. At that moment the tufters came level with the pit, but it so happened some ran above it and some below it, none of them chancing either to scent or see the stag. There the stag stood quite still watching the hounds passing him, realising no doubt that his chance of escaping their notice lay in not moving. So far as all those tufters were concerned the stag was correct, but unfortunately for him one tufter had lagged behind and in following the rest he went straight through the pit. Thereupon he came right on the stag, who then thought it was time to leave.

As pets, wild red deer, whether stags or hinds, are not a success. I have known several instances where they have been caught quite young and brought up on milk from a lamb's tin. For a time all goes well and they are quite gentle. Treated like lambs they will play about the yard and enter the house for food in a delightful way. As they get older, however, they become obstreperous and damage the gardens both of their owner and his neighbours. They are also liable to be danger-ous to children, for when they are in the habit of being fed by hand, they become very insistent for more, and unless it is forthcoming they are apt to strike out with their forefeet or butt as the case may be. Those I have known brought up in this way have had in the end to be killed.

CHAPTER XIII   COMPANIONS IN HARBOURING

FROM time to time some of those who were interested in hunting used to express a wish to see a stag "harboured." The first to accompany me on one of these expeditions was the late Colonel the Hon. Aubrey Herbert of Pixton. Arrangements were made for me to meet Colonel Herbert at the "beech tree," a well-known landmark in Storridge, at 5 a.m. on the morning of a Haddon meet. From that point we could look over Haddon Wood and Hartford Cleeve, where deer can almost any day be seen.

This particular morning, however, turned out to be an exception, and there was nothing to be viewed. Our next move was to Storridge Plantation, above which I knew deer had recently been feeding in a turnip field. On making our way round the outskirts of the plantation we hit off the slots of seven stags, all of which had evidently been lately soiling in a mud pit near by. When these slots had been duly examined and the probable ages of the various deer that made them had been surmised, we traced the slots without difficulty into the plantation. Next came the job of going round the wood to look if there were any slots to be seen that suggested the deer had gone out again. There was none, so satisfied a good stag had been harboured, we rode back to Frogwell Lodge for breakfast. There we found a groom waiting with a fresh horse and some breakfast for Colonel Herbert. At this moment a pleasant smell of fried ham and eggs filled the room, and on this Colonel Herbert discarded his own breakfast and asked if he might share ours. For years afterwards the Colonel would refer to that breakfast as " the best he ever had in his life," an undoubted compliment to the keenness of Somerset morning air. Soon after the meal was finished the hounds arrived, and having already helped in harbouring the stag, Colonel Herbert accompanied the tufters to assist in rousing it. This duly accomplished, I then had the honour of piloting Colonel Herbert over as good a run as anyone need wish, and seeing him complete the day by being in at the kill at Halberton and receiving his first slot. I said " complete " the day, but as Halberton is beyond Tiverton Junction there were in those motorless days still many miles to ride home.

Sir Gilbert Wills (now Lord Dulverton) who was at the time residing at Northmoor, Dulverton, came out with me at a very early hour one morning to harbour a stag for a meet at Hele Bridge. We were not lucky enough to see our stag, but after visiting various feeding grounds we found signs of a good one having been feeding in Hele Bridge Orchard. This stag we successfully slotted into Exe Cleeve, where it was eventually found and gave a good run. The memory of that morning's slotting is often brought to mind by the sight of a silver-mounted hunting crop which his lordship kindly presented to me as a memento of the occasion. Lord Dulverton is a keen supporter of harriers and fox-hounds, as well as stag-hounds, and was at one time Master of the two former. Fishing and shooting have likewise always claimed attention, and in all these sports his lordship is an expert.

Another time it was an Indian Prince who honoured me with his company, the late Maharaja of Jodhpur, then at school at Wellington College, who, with an English tutor and two relatives, twice spent the summer holidays at Emmett's Grange near Simonsbath.

With the Hon. Denzil Fortescue, at whose suggestion the expedition was arranged, we all three set off just before daylight for Prayway Fence, with the idea of looking across Warren Farm to see if there were any deer feeding. Fog and drizzling rain made seeing difficult, but just at dawn we caught sight of a stag jumping a wire fence that separated a turnip field from the forest.

Our next move was to ride as fast as possible round Warren Farm in the hope of being able to see to which part of the North Forest the stag was going, but unfortunately we had only just arrived at the right spot when the fog got suddenly thicker and made it impossible to see anything. After waiting an hour or so with no sign of the fog lifting, the Hon. Denzil Fortescue went home leaving the Maharaja with me. When at last the fog cleared off and there was no stag to be seen, I followed my usual practice of riding down unlikely combes and peering over their sides into the likely ones. In one of the latter into which we peeped I was rewarded by the sight of a pair of horns projecting just above the ferns.

Beckoning to my companion who was a few steps behind, he came forward and peeped over the brow of the combe in the direction in which I pointed. Nothing more than the stag's horns were visible, but by making signs with my arms to resemble the spread of the head I succeeded in conveying my meaning. To my great satisfaction the visitor saw the horns almost at once, which he also signified by signs. He was so pleased at our find that it was only with difficulty I was able to restrain him from dancing with delight. Breakfast was followed by the meet, and my companion then had the further satisfaction of seeing the stag roused.

For Earl Fortescue's kindness and generosity in providing me with food and bed whenever my duties took me in the way of Simonsbath or Castle Hill, I am ever grateful, as I am also to many others in the various districts in which I was called upon to harbour.

To Lord Poltimore also I am greatly indebted for the kindness and assistance always given me in the North Molton district.

For meets at Larkbarrow and Hawkcombe Head there was in the lifetime of the late Mr. Nicholas Snow always a home for me at Oare, and after his death the kindness showed me by Mr. MacDermot in placing a room at my disposal is such that I can never forget it.

In Mr. MacDermot who often came out harbouring with me I had a keen rival. Blessed with good eyesight and assisted by a pair of first-rate binoculars he used to compete as to which of us would see a stag first, and in spite of my long experience it was not infrequently I who had to take second place. At Cloutsham, where John and Walter Lang successively lived, no one could wish for two better hosts, and from both of them also I often received assistance in locating stags.

To all these and many other friends whose names I have not mentioned I tender my heartiest thanks.

Sporting parsons: A good stayer: Sporting doctors: A mixed bag: Famous huntsmen.

AMONG the sporting parsons for whom the West Country has always been renowned, the Rev. " Jack " Russell stood out above all others. He was still hunting when I was a boy, but I do not remember ever to have seen him. Devoted both to fox - hunting and stag - hunting, his " view halloa " is said to have been recognisable by every rustic between Dartmoor and Exmoor. The first meet of stag-hounds the Rev. " Jack " Russell ever attended was on 30th September 1814, at Baron's Down near Dulverton, when the first Earl Fortescue was Master. The horse he rode had been bought at Tiverton Fair on the day before especially for the occasion, and, after three hours' run without a check, it took him to the kill at Slade Bridge below Hawkridge.* He died in his eighty-eighth year, and from hunting with the first Earl Fortescue in 1814 he lived to hunt with and see stags killed during the Mastership (1881-1887) of Lord Ebrington, now the fourth Earl.

Devoted to all forms of hunting it was principally as a Master of Fox-hounds that Russell was chiefly known, but in spite of all the tales told of his

* *Memoir of the Rev. John Russell,* by E. W. L. Davies.

173

sporting proclivities he is said to have been a good friend to the poor and to have left no pastoral duty unperformed.*

Unknown to fame even locally, but none the less good sportsman for that, was the Rev. Cowden Cole, vicar of the tiny village of Upton during the time I was living at Haddon. A minute cottage served as a residence, for the present vicarage was not then built, and alone and unattended the Reverend gentleman lived on a stipend of, I believe, approximately forty pounds a year. On such a tiny income, and so far as I know there were no private means, it may well be wondered how, even in those days of cheap living, hunting was accomplished, for whenever hounds met in the Dulverton district the Rev. Cowden Cole was almost sure to be there. It was managed in this wise. There belonged to a carpenter in Upton an old grey pony of about fourteen hands which was used by its owner for hauling such things as gates and posts that required to be taken away from the shop. On this pony the parson acquired an option for hunting days at five bob a time, to include attendance at the meet and riding in the chase. The pony was not a galloper but it was a stayer, and I can see the old gentleman now, garbed in leggings over his trousers—he never wore breeches

* *Dictionary of National Biography.*

174

—an Inverness cape over his shoulders—never a mackintosh—and a square bowler hat on his head, plodding away behind all the rest. He was always behind, sometimes so far behind that he used to meet the hounds coming back, but I never knew him to give in till news filtered through that the hounds had either killed or abandoned the hunt. One day I remember was very lucky for him. The hounds had gone up the Haddeo Valley after a stag which, after going some distance beyond, turned back to Haddon. The old gentleman as usual was several miles behind, when all of a sudden just as he had reached Hartford the double back on the part of the stag brought him in at the kill. Owing to the unexpected turn events had taken, very few of the Field were present, and when the Master was looking round and considering to whom he should present the slots, I ventured to draw his attention to the devoted sportsman who had so luckily contrived to be on the spot. Thereupon the presentation was made, and I shall never forget the look of pleasure that came over the old gentleman's countenance at the unexpected honour thus befalling him. Beaming all over as he accepted the trophy, he whipped a two-shilling piece out of his pocket for the huntsman, a show of open-hearted generosity he could possibly ill afford.

175

It was always said that at the end of hunting days the grey pony was rewarded with a pint of oats taken from a store of one bushel which the reverend gentleman laid in at the begininng of each season. Doubtless on the evening of that memorable day the pint pot was filled to overflowing.

For many years in succession two clergymen used to spend their holidays together at Minehead, whence they attended all the meets in the district. I do not know their names, but they always wore white coats and were known locally as the " sporting parsons."

From sporting parsons I pass to sporting doctors, and of these the memory of the late Dr. Charles Palk Collyns of Dulverton will ever be associated with the " Devon and Somerset." Born in 1793, Dr. Collyns practised in Dulverton from 1814 to the year of his death in 1864. During his lifetime the Hunt fell on evil times, which followed the sale of the pack in 1825. For two years from this date stag-hunting was in complete abeyance, and after Sir Arthur Chichester had hunted the hounds from 1827-1833 there was another blank of four years until 1837. During these four years the deer were killed so freely by poachers and others interested in their destruction that they were almost exterminated. During this critical period for hunting Dr. Palk Collyns took

176

the matter up, and it was largely through his personal energy that interest was again raised in the sport. A subscription pack, christened the " Devon and Somerset," was the happy result of his efforts, and though many troublous times were still to come, it was mainly through the public-spirited efforts of Dr. Palk Collyns that the foundation of the Hunt's future prosperity was again laid. In his kinsman, Dr. R. J. Collyns— " Dr. Robert " as his patients like to call him— Chairman of the Dulverton Fox Hunt Committee, Dulverton possesses a staunch friend and sportsman to carry on the traditions of his doughty ancestor.

One of the hardest riders to hounds in the West Country and a friend of all sportsmen is Dr. Foster of Porlock, and many are the pleasant chats I have had with him in the old days. He is hunting still, and long may he continue to do so.

Though not much seen in the hunting-field during the latter part of his life, no one could have been keener on sport than the late Dr. G. F. Sydenham of Dulverton. Hunting, shooting, and fishing all came the same to him. At fishing he was an expert both with the fly and clear-water worm, and he has left on record that in 1879, the year so disastrously wet for agriculture and correspondingly good for fishing, he killed no less than 3523 trout, fishing from

February to September.* For knowledge of the moor and its dwellers Dr. Sydenham was excelled by few, and though he did not hunt regularly he often contrived to " drop in " with the hunt when on his rounds. He used to tell a tale of how there once occurred the unusual collection of a red-headed woman, a stag, a fox, and an itinerant brass band all in the same field at the same time. The explanation was as follows : On the edge of the field there was a wayside inn, in front of which a band was playing ; the red-headed woman was carrying out drinks to them ; a hunted stag with the hounds in pursuit selected that moment to cross the field, and in the general hullabaloo a fox, thinking it advisable to shift his quarters, came sneaking down the side of the hedgerow.

To read the history of the " Devon and Somerset " is to learn of famous huntsmen. Of these James Tout held office in the days before the famous pack was sold in 1825. Before him was the celebrated Joe Faulkner who, after a short and chequered career, became whipper-in to his successor, Tout, and again in much later days came Babbage.

The first huntsman I can personally recollect was Arthur Heal who was at the height of his fame when I was a boy. He had been huntsman for

* *Dulverton and the District.* "Homeland Handbooks."

eight years when H.R.H. The Prince of Wales, afterwards King Edward VII, hunted on Exmoor in 1879 and, piloted over the forest by Earl Fortescue and Mr. Chorley, enjoyed a good run. Well do I remember that day, for too young to be taken to the meet myself I had to be content with enviously watching farmers and labourers clamber into crowded wagons which had been commandeered from the hayfields for the great occasion.

Arthur Heal lived to be just on a hundred. Regardless of the Psalmist's views on the allotted span of life he continued to follow the hounds almost up to the time of his death, thereby following the example of many another West Country sportsman to whom old age has few terrors so long as the seat in the saddle still remains firm.

At the time I became harbourer, Anthony Huxtable was in his prime. After him followed Sidney Tucker who had before that been whipper-in. Following Sidney Tucker came Ernest Bawden who is still hunting the hounds to-day. What the skill shown in the olden days may have been I do not know, but I cannot believe four better men than these ever hunted stag-hounds.

179

CHAPTER XV   THE FOREST OF EXMOOR

The forest of Exmoor: The Doone Valley at dawn: A night ride over Dunkery: Soft ground: Surface gutters: Empty saddles: Bog land: An unpleasant experience: Exmoor sheep: Shepherds and sheep dogs: Wild ponies: Some horses I have ridden.

THE term "forest," used in its ancient and legal sense does not imply the presence of woods but signifies a district in which deer and other wild animals were placed under "forest" laws.

There might or might not be woods on a "forest," and the forest of Exmoor as it exists to-day is practically devoid of trees, though some of the wooded areas now on its borders once came within its boundaries. Until Mr. John Knight bought the Forest rather more than a hundred years ago, and with his son, Sir Frederick, who followed him, reclaimed many hundreds of acres and built houses and roads, the moor had undergone little change, and there are still parts of it such as the Chains and the North and South Forest which, except for a few fences and drainage gutters, remain in much the same state as they were in the earliest times.

The moor appears to have been a Royal forest from early days, and tradition says that Saxon kings hunted over it from Porlock. There is, however, said to be no direct evidence of kings hunting there at any later date, though venison was doubtless obtained from it for Royal use when required. Among the quarry mentioned in licences granted to notable personages to hunt other animals than deer, are the fox, badger and wild cat. The first of these is still very plentiful, and the badger is by no means uncommon, but I have never heard of anyone who had seen a wild cat. Of the larger birds, buzzards and herons are numerous, and ravens are by no means rare. The experiment of introducing grouse on Exmoor first made by Sir Edward Mountain promises to be successful, but blackgame that were formerly so plentiful have for some reason or other become quite scarce. Of all the hours for visiting the moor none can beat the early morning. To stand at the top of the Doone Valley and look down on the " waterslide " flowing smoothly to the bottom of the hillside like a sheet of unbroken glass, is an experience I should be sorry to have missed. From overhead come the cries of buzzards and curlews, and withal the sense of loneliness is often such that even the bleating of a sheep brings relief.

One of the worst predicaments I ever was in resulted from an attempt to ride over the moor by night. On the day previous to a Cloutsham meet, a shooting party at Haddon prevented me from leaving home so early as I should otherwise have done. So far as the actual harbouring was concerned I did not worry, because the Langs with whom I was to stay the night at Cloutsham would, I knew, help me with that.

With the short October days—for there was no "summer time" then—it was dusk before I started, and by the time I arrived at Dunkery Gate it was quite dark. Foolishly, I there decided to take the shorter way over the hill by the path I generally used, instead of going the somewhat longer but surer way by the road. It was by this time too dark to see anything, so trusting to my horse to find the way I gave him his head and off we started. For a while all went on swimmingly and I was beginning to congratulate myself on the excellent progress we were making, when all of a sudden my horse went down and pitched me over its head. Gathering myself together and finding no bones were broken, I began to explore the surroundings, and after some groping round I came to the conclusion we must have missed our way and tumbled into a gully which we ought to have gone over at a level crossing lower down. By stretching my arm up the gully sides I could just feel the heather on the top, from which I judged the depth to be rather more than my own height and too great to think of trying to clamber out. The darkness was intense, and to make matters worse two matches were all my pockets could produce, for in the hurry of leaving I had forgotten to bring a new box. I gingerly struck one of them, and a puff of wind immediately blew it out. The second burnt a little better and lasted just long enough for me to see and grab hold of my horse. Having got my bearings to this point the only thing to do was to work my way down the gully until we came to a place where the sides shelved sufficiently to allow us to get out. Fortunately the season had been a dry one, and there was no water to contend with. Slowly backing my horse downwards, I kept in touch with the surroundings by tapping the ground and sides of the gully with my hunting crop as I went along. Finally I struck on a soft patch which I took to be the spot at which we ought to have crossed had we kept to the path.

Once on the hillside again I felt more at ease, but I had had quite enough riding for that night, and leading my horse we started to walk up the hill. That was a moment when I could have wished someone would light the beacon like the Doones did when John Fry and Jan Ridd were crossing Dunkery on their way to Oare, for it was pitch dark, and I was anything but sure of the right direction.

To my great relief the sensation of walking uphill, to which I was largely trusting, gave way at last to that of going downhill, by which I judged we were over the top, an opinion that not long afterwards was confirmed by the sight of a distant light swinging to and fro. Long blasts on my whistle soon attracted the attention of Walter Lang, for alarmed by my non-appearance it was he who had turned out with a lantern on the chance of guiding me. In a few more minutes I was at Cloutsham Farm, and the pleasure of sitting once more in a comfortable chair before a blazing fire, after a long day's shoot, followed by a toss over my horse's head and a weary walk over Dunkery in the dark, was very great. Had the weather not been fine I might have had a different story to tell, for, as I know to my cost, Dunkery can be very awful in a storm. With a meet at Slowley on one day and another at Larkbarrow on the next, I had arranged, in order to harbour for both meets, to go from Chargot Lodge at Luxborough on to Oare, where I was to stay with the late Mr. Nicholas Snow. Rain was already falling in torrents when I started, and the wind was blowing a gale. My first attempt was to cross Dunkery by the Codsend Fence, but my horse refused to face the weather and I was forced to drop down over Sweetery where there was more shelter. Finally it became impossible to reach Oare that evening, so I stayed at Cloutsham Farm. The next morning when I had to be out at dawn looking for a stag, the storm had abated, and the harbouring fortunately turned out to be simple. As soon as the pack had been laid on I lost no time in starting for the eighteen miles' ride home, and very glad I was to get there !

As the elements are sometimes treacherous so also is the ground, and few of those habitually hunting over the moor can say they have never been caught napping. The grass that looks so friendly on the surface is not always all it seems.

Even in dry weather large tracts of the moor are always soft, especially round about Pinford and the Chains, a "ten minutes' scurry" over the neighbourhood of which, as Mr. Philip Everard* aptly puts it, "seems to effect a wonderful change in the ideas of the majority of the Field," and there saddles, including my own, have been emptied more times than I should care to count.

What are known as "surface gutters" which are open drains, are particularly dangerous, for blown by the wind, the sedge grass growing alongside them lies almost flat on their surfaces. This makes it difficult for horses to see where the gutters lie, and as some of these gutters are from

* *Stag-hunting with the Devon and Somerset.*

three to four feet deep a horse unexpectedly plunging into one is almost sure to go down. Scores of times, when riding over the moor, I have heard water running down the gutters without being able to see their whereabouts on account of the grass hiding them from view.

Nevertheless it is surprising how well horses accustomed to the moor instinctively learn to avoid them. I fancy they see the grass at the edges of the gutters sinking somewhat away, and, with a keen appreciation of what is beneath, they jump the drains and land their riders in safety.

Besides soil that is only " soft," there are here and there considerable tracts of more definite bog land, across parts of which it is often impossible to ride. These bogs which are chiefly in the region of Pinford and the Chains are doubtless the foundation of Blackmore's realistic description of the " Wizard's Slough " into which Jan Ridd threw Carver Doone. Though very disconcerting to those who land in them these bogs are fortunately seldom really dangerous. I have heard of a horse being engulfed in them, but have never myself known of any fatality happening to a rider. There is, however, a tradition that Mole's Chamber, marked on some old maps as a " dangerous bog," is called after a Mr. Mole who, with his horse, is said to have perished there.

HERD OF STAGS ON THE FOREST

The worst experience of the kind I ever witnessed was not upon the moor itself, and occurred at a spot where I should never have thought of it happening. There was a meet at Crowcombe Heathfield Station, and I had slotted stags from a clover field into Combe Wood near Lydeard St. Lawrence, a covert into which I had never previously been. When it came to tufting, Sidney Tucker and I entered the wood at the lower end, and, like me, Sidney had never been there before. On the tufters giving tongue and starting at a fast pace to go through the wood towards Crowcombe coverts, we galloped as fast as we could along a wide path leading in the same direction. Sidney was leading by about thirty yards when his horse suddenly struck a soft patch and fell, throwing its rider clean over its head. Pulling up only just in time to prevent my own horse sharing the same fate, I jumped out of the saddle and ran to Sidney's assistance. Quickly extricating him from the soft ground in which his face was embedded, I freed his nose and mouth from mud sufficiently to allow him to breathe. After that he had to be made presentable, the making of which I took a part in scraping him down and washing his face with my pocket handkerchief dipped in the water from a neighbouring spring. The horse started to plunge and managed to extricate himself all right. After putting some final touches to both of them, Sidney got into the saddle again. None the worse for his adventure, he proceeded to ride on after his hounds, which he found had been stopped at Crowcombe Heathfield in order to find out the cause of his absence. For my part, my work being over, I proceeded to ride slowly in the direction of home. There was, however, still more for me to see that day, for on stopping at Willett Wood and looking across to Crowcombe Coverts to see if there were any signs of the hounds, the stag passed close by me. It was followed by one of the tufters which the Whip had failed to stop, and this had evidently been making hunting difficult for the rest of the pack, as it always does if one or more of the hounds are running on the scent a long way in front of the rest. I stopped this hound, and as soon as the huntsman came in sight signalled to him to come on. After that point, up to which hunting had been slow, hounds went straight ahead with scarcely a check until reaching the River Exe near Winsford, where there ended as good a run as one need wish for.

For sheep, the moor provides large tracts of excellent summer pasture, and the Exmoor horned variety are noted both for their strong constitution and the qualities of their mutton and wool. The shepherds who live on the moor have naturally many opportunities for knowing the whereabouts of deer, and often gave me information that was very acceptable. William Little, who hailed from Scotland and who, with his two sons, shepherded a Cheviot flock for Earl Fortescue, I often used to meet at the boundary gate between Larkbarrow and Oare Common, where the dividing line ran between the properties of Earl Fortescue and ʻMr. Snow. The news he would on these occasions bring me about stags was often very useful in determining the best position for me to take up the next morning for seeing the deer returning from their feeding grounds.

A cup of tea and bite of bread were also much appreciated by an appetite keenly sharpened in the moorland air, and I still recollect how good were the home-baked loaves he used on these occasions to produce. Little owned two beautiful collies which gave me an unexpected experience of their abilities that I have never forgotten. We were standing by the boundary gate one day as usual and talking about three stags that were in the habit of frequenting Pinford, while the two dogs were lying on the bank behind us. After telling me all about the deer, Little went on to say : " I've lost a sheep somewhere. I'm afraid it's strayed on Mr. Snow's side. If it has, the

189

horned sheep will be sure to butt it in the head and make its eyes swell so that it can't see to get back." The lost sheep to which he referred was one of the Cheviots which Earl Fortescue always kept, and for some little time he continued to lament the loss and explain how he had looked everywhere without success. While we were thus talking, I suddenly interrupted the conversation. " I can hear dogs barking behind us now," I said. We turned to face the direction from which the sound came, and as we did so I noticed the two dogs which had been lying on the bank behind us were no longer there. Little listened. " Them's my dogs," he stated. " They must have been and found my sheep."

" Your dogs could never pick out the sheep you've lost from all those sheep belonging to Mr. Snow," I retorted incredulously, as I gazed at the flocks browsing on the moor in front of me. " I'll bet they've found my sheep," was the firm reply, and on that he started to walk towards the sound of barking.

Not believing any dogs could pick out a sheep like that, I rode by his side determined to see what it was all about.

Little still continued to repeat, " they'd found his sheep," and on reaching the edge of Stowey's Combe and looking down, sure enough in the hollow we saw Little's two dogs trying their utmost to drive a sheep along in our direction. I still accompanied the shepherd to make sure it was the Cheviot sheep the dogs had, and this, when we got there, it proved to be. As we had expected, the Exmoor horned sheep had battered its face so that it was unable to see.

Picking it up and throwing it over his shoulder in the skilful manner of shepherds, Little triumphantly brought back his lost one to the fold.

Scent is such a powerful factor with dogs that for all I know the smell of a Cheviot sheep may differ from an Exmoor variety as plainly as " chalk from cheese," but even so, how did those dogs, which were lying quietly on the bank when we began to talk, know the sheep was lost, and why did they choose that particular moment to go off to find it ? Did they in some remarkable way suddenly scent it, or did they, as seems just possible, from Little's somewhat animated use of the word " sheep " and " lost "—words no doubt they had been in the habit of hearing in their commands—take it as a bidding to go and find it ?

In whatever way the idea may have been conveyed to them it struck me as a marvellous piece of work, though I am bound to say that the shepherd did not appear to be greatly surprised at what the dogs had done.

A fascinating feature of the moor are the wild ponies which find their own " keep " on the heather and grass. They are quite small, averaging about twelve hands, and very hardy. When young and unbroken they are full of mettle, but well handled they become quite docile and can be made into serviceable pets for children to ride. Every year they are rounded up and sent in droves to Bampton Fair. In former days they fetched good prices, but in this mechanised age little use is found for them and they can be bought for a song. Recent years have seen the formation of a society for preserving and furthering the breed, in which Earl Fortescue, Mr. R. V. Le Bas of Winsford and Dr. R. J. Collyns of Dulverton have taken prominent parts. Through this society prizes are offered at Horse Shows for the best entries.

A good horse is a great ally to a harbourer. Scores of times my attention has been drawn to the presence of deer near by, by my horse pricking up his ears and staring in the direction of the deer which he has been able to scent. Of many good horses that have passed through my hands, I think the best was one called the " Mount." It was called after the house of that name at Dulverton where Mr. A. B. Hill, who made me a present of the horse, then lived. It was always willing and never gave me a fall, though I must have ridden him thousands of miles. Another favourite was a chestnut mare I bought from the late Dr. G. F. Sydenham. For many years she carried me well, and there was scarcely any part of the country we did not go over together. Considering the number of falls I have had at one time or another, including one in the Iron Mill Valley near Chain Bridge when my horse twice rolled over me, I have been extraordinarily lucky in never breaking any bones. The commonest cause of falls on the moor are soft patches into which the horse unexpectedly puts its feet and sends the rider over its head. Times out of number I have seen this happen, fortunately as a rule with wonderfully little injury beyond damage to smart clothes. The peaty soil is terrible stuff to stain, and breeches of spotless white in the morning often assume a far more sombre hue towards night.

To be riding a horse that suddenly stops in the dark and refuses to move, gives a queer sensation and makes one wonder what is going to happen next. While riding along a narrow lane leading to the moor one morning before it was light my horse suddenly stopped and snorted at something he evidently disliked. Unable to get him to budge and it being too dark to see anything, I dismounted and explored the roadway in front by means of my hunting-crop. Two or three yards ahead I could hear the sound of heavy breathing, and on getting close to it I found a man lying across the road. From his appearance he had evidently been there all night, and after a good deal of shaking and shouting he recovered from his torpor—due apparently to drink—sufficiently to be able to walk away.

CHAPTER XVI   OLD TIMES AND NEW

Old customs: Venison feasts: A pleasant substitute: Exford Horse Show: A subterfuge and its sequel: Dulverton and stag-hunting: Dulverton Fair.

IN stag-hunting as in other affairs of life, many customs that are interesting to read about have long since passed away. Some no doubt have gone for the better, and some possibly for worse. In his *Chase of the Wild Red Deer*, Dr. Palk Collyns tells us of gay times of long ago. How, at Castle Hill, from 1812-1818 with Earl Fortescue as Master, a successful day finished with the entry of the huntsman in full hunting kit into the dining-room, where, after prosperity to stag-hunting had been toasted, he sounded the " *morte*."

Those, too, were the times when big hunting festivities required toasts to be drunk from a silver cup fixed in the stag's mouth, the whole head being tilted to the necessary angle by grasping the stag's horns. This custom I believe survived for a long time in some parts, but it had entirely gone out before anything I can remember.

Still earlier in history we learn that those who hunted and left before the deer was killed were fined, an unpleasant outlook for some who like to take their sport less seriously.

Gone likewise are the days when the dates of meets were given out in churches and when " As pants the hart" was regularly sung on the first Sunday in every season, to be followed on one occasion by an eloquent sermon based on the text: "Lo, we heard of the same in Ephrata and found it in the wood."

Among old-time customs that have gone out in my own day are the "Venison Feasts." At the bidding of the Master, these popular institutions were held in October at the end of every stag-hunting season. To begin with there was one held at Dulverton and one at Porlock, but in later years one was also held at North Molton. The guests included all the farmers and other deer preservers in the neighbourhood of each "Feast," and punctually at six o'clock in the evening the Master, supported by the Hon. Secretary and other members of the Hunt Committee, took the chair.

A mighty onslaught on the haunch of venison and other good provender so generously provided, quickly put everybody in good humour for further gaiety to come. This began, after the loyal toasts had been honoured, with "Prosperity to Stag-hunting!" Proposed by the Master and replied to by hunting farmers, it was joyfully drunk in piping hot punch ladled out at the Master's table.

By this time the party, which often numbered from one hundred to two hundred guests, was in merry mood. Songs and speeches followed each other in rapid succession, until, at a late hour of the night or an early hour in the morning, the last strains of such favourites as *John Peel* and *Uncle Tom Cobleigh and All* gradually faded away and the guests made up their minds to go home.

In place of these " Feasts " which are no longer held in their old form, Colonel Wiggin, the present Master of the " Devon and Somerset," generously provides a very pleasing substitute in the sumptuous luncheon to which he invites the farmers and deer preservers on the occasion of the Exford Horse Show. This annual institution, which was inaugurated originally by Earl Fortescue in 1885, has become one of the important sporting events of the West Country year.

By the harbourer, all such merrymaking must be enjoyed with due care, lest he oversleep himself on the following morning when he must harbour a stag for the meet that almost invariably follows on the day after a social sporting event. On the other hand, it would never do to rule sociability altogether out, and in order not to appear ungrateful for hospitality often so generously offered, I must plead guilty to having more than once arranged for my glass to be refilled with water after the first drink. In one district I used to visit, the overwhelming kindness of my friends made this subterfuge necessary each time I went there, and led some years afterwards to an amusing sequel. On the afternoon before the day of the meet in that particular neighbourhood it was the custom of several of the sporting farmers living around to meet me on my arrival at the inn at which I always put up for the night.

Over our hunting talk and the information they were able to give me as to the whereabouts in the district stags were lying—information the value of which I greatly appreciated—hospitality in the shape of whisky was generously and lavishly pressed upon me. Not wishing to seem churlish in not responding to such well-meant kindness, but realising the necessity for strict abstemiousness with the harbouring in front of me, I took an opportunity of taking the landlord aside and arranging the subterfuge I have described above.

As round followed round I solemnly placed my glass in the niche on the mantel shelf and bravely drank my share. When this pleasant jollification had lasted for an hour or two, and my friends were preparing to leave for home, I used to fancy they sometimes looked a little surprised at the ease with which I appeared to be carrying my share. Some two or three years after I had given up harbouring I happened to be attending a sheep fair where I chanced to meet an old friend who invited me to walk with him to his motor car and have a drink. On the way we met several of the old acquaintances who were so lavish in their hospitality on my visits to the inn. My friend asked them to join us, and we all went on together. When we got to the car, and the whisky was being poured into my glass to the accompaniment of the usual question " Say when ? " I replied by asking for a modest amount. At this the others burst into loud laughter.

" Don't you worry about that," said one of them to my host, " he's the smartest fellow to drink whisky I've ever come across. We've often tried to down him at —— and *we've* never been able to do it."

Dulverton, near to which I have all my life lived, has from ancient times always been a great centre for stag-hunting. From 1740-1746 Mr. Edward Dyke of Pixton and Holnicote was Master, and after him followed Sir Thomas Dyke Acland who also resided at Pixton.

In those days the hounds were kennelled at Jury at the top of the hill above Hele Bridge and conveniently close to Pixton Park.

Presumably hounds were at some time or other also kept at Pixton itself, for when alterations to outbuildings were being carried out there a few years ago, the remains of old cooking furnaces and an ancient cobble floor with a primitive drainage scheme were unearthed, the whole at some time or other having seemingly served as a feeding house for hounds.

When the hounds were kept at Castle Hill from 1812-1818 they used to lie out at Higher Combe between Dulverton and Winsford for meets on the Dulverton side, and at Porlock for that side of the country. Later on Mr. Stucley Lucas was Master, and kept the hounds at Baron's Down near Dulverton, and it was after he ceased to be Master in 1825 that hunting fell on bad times and the pack was sold. Of these hounds which had been bred especially for stag-hunting and as a breed had been in the country for a very long time, Dr. Palk Collyns says no man ever saw a nobler pack.

In 1855 after the Hunt had been again placed on a firmer footing, Pixton once more became the centre, when Mr. Fenwick Bisset, who was then residing there, took over the Mastership and kennelled the pack at Jury. During Mr. Bisset's long Mastership over the long term of twenty-six years, the fortunes of the Hunt, which had been varying since 1825, took an upward turn, though another period of ill-luck occurred at the end of the 'seventies, when the pack developed rabies.

When Mr. Bisset resigned in 1880 he was succeeded by Lord Ebrington (now Earl Fortescue) who was Master for six seasons and to whose wisdom in electing to kill a large number of deer and so to allay much discontent from the damage they were doing, allusion has been previously made.

Lord Ebrington was succeeded by Mr. C. H. Basset, and after him came Colonel Hornby, the first Master under whom I had the honour to serve.

The old time glories of Dulverton Fair had departed before my time. It began on 10th July, and I have always been interested in hearing that the local farm labourers were in the habit of buying their scythe stones there. If that is any indication of the date at which cutting grass then commenced farmers were either much later in beginning than they are to-day or the seasons were different. In this neighbourhood we reckon to start cutting grass about the twentieth of June, though the date on the forest is naturally somewhat later. Anyone in this part who postponed the cutting until near mid-July would be called, as we say locally, an " afternoon " farmer.

CHAPTER XVII   WAR-TIME AND AFTER

CLOUTSHAM BALL, on the summit of which stands
Cloutsham Farm, is the place where the opening
meet is always held. To this rule I can remember
only two exceptions. The first occurred when I
was a boy and the meet was held at Holm Bush
Gate, Porlock Hill, on account of the recent death
of Mr. Bisset, who first started the practice of
holding opening meets at Cloutsham. The second
occasion was when I was harbourer, and the meet
was then held at Haddon instead of Cloutsham
out of respect for the death of the late Sir Thomas
Dyke Acland. Though standing at a considerable
altitude Cloutsham Ball lies somewhat in a hollow,
being overshadowed by Dunkery on one side and
the steeply rising Horner Woods on the other.
The latter always hold deer which also like to lie
amongst the rough bracken on the side of the Ball.
The steepness of the hillsides thereabouts makes
riding to hounds difficult, but much to make the
going easier has been accomplished by Sir Francis
Acland and the late Sir Thomas Acland who,
though not riding to hounds themselves, have

202

caused old paths to be trimmed and new ones to be made, thereby in this and other ways adding greatly to the welfare of the Hunt.

For large numbers of people, especially on that side of the country, " Cloutsham " means a general holiday, and being held in the first week in August the meet naturally attracts large numbers of visitors from the seaside and other resorts around. Before the days of motors every sort of vehicle, from donkey cart to four-in-hand, used to assemble there, but, in consequence of the inaccessible and narrow roads, motor cars have to be left either at Webbers Post or Stoke Ridge. Both these spots are, however, excellent for sightseers, and a view of the " lay on " and a sight of the stag can often be obtained from them. Many are the strange questions I have been asked about stag-hunting on these days. Quite unaware of my identity one of two young men talking to me summed up my duties very quickly. " What are the duties of the harbourer ? " asked one. Before I could reply, his friend answered for me. " Why, don't you know ? " he said, " the harbourer is the man who rides to the meet, tells the Master where to draw, and blows a whistle." Of regular stag-hunters, many can count their opening meets in scores, but I fancy Mr. Christopher Birmingham, past Agent for the Holnicote Estate, with an attendance for sixty seasons without a break, must hold the record for the present day.

Of all the meets at Cloutsham I have myself attended, that of 5th August 1914 will always be the most memorable. On arriving at Cloutsham that morning many were still uncertain of the way the affairs of the nation had gone. At the meet, authentic news quickly came. Punctually to the minute Major Morland Greig arrived, and, reining up his horse alongside the huntsman and hounds, addressed the huge crowd of which he formed the centre. In a few words he told us that war had been declared, and in consequence the meet and all future hunting would be cancelled until further notice. For a few seconds there was silence. Then at a word from Major Greig, heads were bared, and " God Save the King " was sung with a fervour I never expect to hear the like of again.

That was the last time I ever saw Major Greig. He left immediately afterwards to join his regiment, and to the sorrow of the whole countryside news came in 1915 of his death at Gallipoli. A more energetic and sporting Master never followed hounds.

In the difficult times that were to come, Earl Fortescue's intimate knowledge of all pertaining to hounds and hunting, helped in many a difficult situation as it had done so often before and as it continues to do to-day, for as Chairman of the Hunt, his lordship never fails to take an active interest in the chase. With this influence behind it, the Committee, through an executive consisting of Mr. Froude Hancock, Mr. Philip Everard, and Mr. H. G. Thornton, at that time Hon. Secretary to the Hunt, kept the organisation intact and prevented things coming to a standstill. To all of which the late Mr. Badco also gave invaluable help and he was, on the death of Major Morland Greig, appointed Master. On the resignation of Mr. Badco, after the cessation of the War, Colonel Wiggin, well known for many years in the West Country for the interest he had taken in stag-hunting, was appointed Master and holds office at the present day. Under his able and genial guidance things soon pulled together again. One of his first actions was to introduce the breeding of hounds at Exford, for, with packs depleted throughout the country on account of the War, a supply of suitable drafts from fox-hounds could no longer be relied on. The experiment thus begun has turned out to be a great success, and ably backed by the huntsman, Ernest Bawden, Colonel Wiggin spares neither time nor expense to improve the quality of the pack which has now reached a very high standard of efficiency.

Farmers and other sportsmen around readily take the puppies out to " walk " until they are a year old when they are returned to the Kennels. Every year, about June, a puppy show is held in the Master's grounds at Exford, and valuable prizes, given by Colonel and Mrs. Wiggin, are awarded to the best dog and bitch puppies that have been " walked." A more popular Master than Colonel Wiggin it would be difficult to find, and whoever succeeds him will not find his footsteps easy ones in which to follow.

Among townspeople there seems to be a general idea that stag-hunting and indeed all forms of hunting are sports only for the " idle rich." This certainly does not apply to the West Country where I have lived all my life. Far from emphasising class distinction, stag-hunting produces a sense of good fellowship that most other sports would find hard to beat. Those who can afford to ride horses form only a part of the total numbers to whom stag-hunting gives some of the greatest pleasure in their lives.

Of the motors that attend the meets many are hired by local enthusiasts with money saved specially for the occasion. Next come the cyclists, and after them the crowds that enjoy themselves on " shanks' " ponies.

Nor must it be thought that all these onlookers

come out of curiosity or as mere sightseers. Included among them are some of the keenest stag-hunters in the West Country, and though they follow only on foot, there is little that most of the riders could tell them about stag-hunting they do not already know. On days when the scent is poor, the more experienced of them often help the huntsman with information as to the wiles they may have seen the stag carrying out, and with a keen sense of direction and locality they often contrive to be in at the end of a run.

There is nothing the people of the countryside like better than to be able to help the Hunt, and to take temporary charge of a straying hound gives pleasure no end. They are proud to have the chance of helping such a hound, and will look after it and often share their meals with it until it can be safely returned. I once knew a sporting post-man who, on meeting with a stray hound, tried to coax it to follow him. Not meeting with a very ready response, the postman, remembering a pound of sausages he had been commissioned to bring home for supper, tried bribery. Taking a sausage from his pocket he gave it to the hound. The effect of this was excellent for a time but finding no more forthcoming the hound began to lag behind again. Another sausage was therefore required and still another. . . . One by one they were gradually doled out, but as the last of them disappeared, the postman, supperless but triumphant, had the satisfaction of marching into Dulverton with the hound safely at his heels. At the present time I know an old man of eighty-four who has worked hard all his life and never ridden a horse hunting, but who still never misses going to a local meet. He must have run hundreds and hundreds of miles after hounds in his lifetime. At this stage he is still a stayer, and can often be seen wending his way up the Barle Valley on the chance of seeing sport.

Another old man round about ninety is scarcely less enthusiastic, while among the seventies there are many whose pace younger men might envy.

On 14th October 1921, when I harboured the last stag of the season for a meet at Wootton Courtney between Minehead and Porlock, I was, quite unknown to myself, officially harbouring for the " Devon and Somerset " for the last time. Before the onset of the New Year, my Master, the late Colonel the Hon. Aubrey Herbert, asked me to become Sub-Agent to the Pixton Estate in place of Mr. Allan, who was retiring after many years' service. This offer, which I gratefully accepted, made it impossible to continue harbouring, and I therefore sent in my resignation, which was duly accepted. On taking up my new duties

I moved from the keeper's cottage in Crewses Meadow into the Sub-Agent's house, also at Weir.

In making this move, a distance of only a few hundred yards, I passed from the parish of King's Brompton, in which I had hitherto always lived, into the parish of Dulverton, the river Exe forming the dividing line between the two.

This new chapter of my life, which so unexpectedly opened out before me, was but one more instance of the innumerable kindnesses and opportunities for advancement I have invariably received at the hands of the late Colonel the Hon. Aubrey Herbert, M.P., of Pixton, and from the Hon. Mrs. Aubrey Herbert. To both, I owe more than I can ever express.

APPENDIX

Included by the courtesy of " West Somerset Free Press "
(October, 1922)

" DEVON AND SOMERSET STAG-HOUNDS "

A HANDSOME PRESENTATION TO FRED GOSS

Tributes to a Good Sportsman

THERE was a big muster near the Keeper's Cot on Winsford Hill on Saturday morning to do honour to Fred Goss, whose long and valued services as harbourer to the Hunt terminated last season. Happily the occasion was free from any of the regrets associated with farewells or infirmities. To-day Goss (to whom the title of " Mr." would sound strange in the hunting-field) is the embodiment of vigorous health and cheerfulness, with many a prospective hunt in store. His appointment to a position of trust on the Carnarvon estate will necessarily make him a less familiar figure in the saddle than hitherto, but it will at the same time enable him to maintain a helpful interest in the sport which he has served with such distinction. His record during the twenty-eight years he held the post of harbourer is familiar to every stag-hunter. Following in the footsteps of Jim Blackmore and Andrew Miles, his skill in woodcraft quickly established him as one of the most trusted and valuable of the Hunt servants.

He was pleasingly reminded of this on Saturday when from far and wide followers of the chase assembled to add their personal tribute to previous marks of appreciation in a more tangible form. Their collective good wishes were expressed in the form of a cheque for over three hundred guineas, which Earl Fortescue (Chairman of the Hunt Committee and a former Master of the pack) had the pleasure of handing to Goss on Saturday. There was much animation when Ernest Bawden, the popular huntsman, sounded the assembly, mounted folk and footpeople forming up in horseshoe fashion with his lordship, Colonel W. W. Wiggin (the Master), Mr. H. G. Thornton (secretary), and Goss, all mounted, in silhouette on the open side.

Among those out were Mrs. Wiggin, the Countess Fortescue, Miss Cust, Mrs. and Miss Thornton, Mr. P. Everard and Mrs. Thomas, Mr. R. B. Magor and Miss W. Magor, Miss Chadwyck-Healey, Mr. and Mrs. O. N. Chadwyck-Healey,

Mr. and Mrs. G. St. C. Pilcher, Miss Waters, Miss Hughes, Miss Harley, Mr. and Mrs. P. F. Hancock, Mr. F. Blofeld, Mr. and Mrs. R. V. Le Bas, Mr. and Mrs. C. M. Houlder, Mr. and Mrs. F. Beadle, Captain Kinglake, M.H., Miss Harford, Mr. Tweed (of the Pytchley), Mrs. Greene, Mrs. Blacker Douglass, Mr. and Mrs. Lovys, Mrs. Froude Bellew, Captain Godfrey Lawson, Major Scarfe, Major Warren, Mrs. Holland, Captain C. B. St. J. Mildmay and the Misses Mildmay, Mr. E. G. C. Chapman, Colonel W. Hartley Maud, C.M.G., Mrs. Maud, and Miss Sneyd, Mr. E. L. Hancock, Colonel H. W. H. Amory, Colonel R. M. Dodington and the Misses Dodington, Mr. and the Misses Browning, Mr. S. Adams and party, Mr. E. C. Lloyd, Mr. and Mrs. F. Willoughby Hancock, Mr. R. A. Bevan, Dr. R. J. Collyns, Mr. R. Greig, Mr. and Mrs. R. V. Awdry, Miss MacLennan, Mr. James Hope, M.P., Mr. and Mrs. G. Morel, Mr. and Mrs. Jack Hill, Mr. Roy Spicer, Mr. and Mrs. Peleran, Mr. L. R. D. Anderson, Mr. H. Russell Thomas, Miss Fitzgerald (Dublin), Mr. and Mrs. J. P. Goddard and Miss Goddard, Mr. C. Evered, Mr. James Tapp, Mr. D. J. Tapp, Mr. and Mrs. Wallis Wilson, Mr. T. H. Rawle, Mr. T. Boucher, Mr. F. G. Heal (Quarme Harriers), Mr. G. Williams, Miss and Master Williams (Wick), Mr. T. C. Pearse, Mr. W. Pring, Mr. R. Stephens (Luckyard), Mr.

EARL FORTESCUE MAKING THE PRESENTATION TO FRED GOSS

MEMORIES OF A STAG HARBOURER

E. C. Rawle (Bossington), Mr. T. Pugsley (Broford), Messrs. W. Pulsford, T. Thorne, F. Thomas, W. Arscott, and E. Bawden (Wiveliscombe), Mr. F. Hayes (Nethercott), Mr. H. J. N. Eames (Dunster), Mr. S. Heywood (Hinam), Mr. T. Michell (Howtown), Miss Gregory (Ashwick), Messrs. W. Dart, T. Price, F. W. Dullingham, E. L. Barker, and —. Catford (Dulverton), Mr. H. Lovibond (Williton), Mr. Vicary (Winsford), Mrs. Heywood, Mr. W. Norman (Steart), Mr. Jack Norman, Mr. and Mrs. E. B. Knight (Clayford), Mr. F. Clatworthy (Stockham), Mr. Sidney Tucker (ex-huntsman of the pack), Ned Lang (harbourer), etc.

RECOGNITION OF WORK WELL DONE

Lord Fortescue, addressing the company, said it was his pleasant task that morning to hand to Fred Goss a cheque for more than three hundred guineas, subscribed for by upwards of six hundred people who wished to offer him a token of their goodwill on his relinquishing the post of harbourer —(applause). A good many of the people who came out with the Hunt earlier in the season took the finding of a stag as much for granted as the eggs and bacon they had for breakfast, knowing little of the difficulties of the harbourer's task or of the woodcraft and the hard work without which the day's sport would not even begin.

But the number of people, residents and visitors, who had joined in making the presentation went to show that there were many who did appreciate the importance of the harbourer's office—(hear, hear). It was rather a remarkable thing that from 1855, when Mr. Bisset put the pack on a sure foundation, up to last year there had only been three regular harbourers. The first was Jim Blackmore, a man highly skilled, who died before his (Lord Fortescue's) time. On one occasion that "wonderful old hound," as Mr. Bisset described him in his diary, after the tufters had drawn a cover blank hit off the slot of a stag and himself hunted the line right up to its bed. Blackmore came to the sport late in life and was succeeded by Andrew Miles, a Hampshire man, who loved the chase and was constantly in at the finish after having been out since daylight. Had Miles been brought up in the kennels instead of as a gamekeeper he would have made an excellent huntsman. After nearly thirty years of excellent work, he died towards the end of Mr. Basset's Mastership, and for a couple of years there was a reversion to the thoroughly unsatisfactory method of harbouring being done by the supposed expert of the locality. Then, in the second year of his Mastership Colonel Hornby was fortunate enough to secure the services of Goss.

MEMORIES OF A STAG HARBOURER

SIR ROBERT SANDERS' HIGH TRIBUTE

The following season Mr. Sanders (as he then was) succeeded to the Mastership, and this was what he had written to him (Lord Fortescue) respecting Goss :

" Will you tell Fred how very sorry I am to miss this opportunity of doing him honour. I should like to have thanked him again for the large share he had in whatever sport I was able to show when I had the hounds. His skill in woodcraft is known to all ; but what was even more valuable to the Master was that he had the courage to be absolutely truthful. On the rare occasions when he was not sure he was not afraid to say so. Consequently when he was sure I could stake the chance of sport for the day on what he said ; and I don't think he ever let me down. I shall always be grateful to him as one of the best helpmates a man could have, and, if I may say so, one of the nicest fellows I ever met "—(applause).

OTHER SERVICES TO THE HUNT

Continuing, Lord Fortescue said he could add little to what had been stated in the letter. Courage and truth, added to diligence and skill, would carry a man a long way in most occupations, but there were two services not alluded to in the letter which Goss did the Hunt, and which ought not to pass unmentioned. In conjunction mainly with Sir Robert Sanders, Goss established the principle that there should be one harbourer, who was as much a part of the Hunt establishment as the huntsman or the whip—(applause). Previous Masters had been trying for that, and he (Lord Fortescue) had purposely associated Goss with Sir Robert in alluding to the appointment, as, if the new man had not added tact and courtesy and good humour to his keen eyesight and his knowledge of woodcraft, the principle of one harbourer for the whole country could never have been established—(applause). Nor was that the only service Goss had rendered the country. Eight years ago, when the War broke out, the number of deer in the country was so great as to cause a great deal of concern. The small committee, consisting of Mr. Hancock, Mr. Everard and himself, who in the absence of the Master (Major Greig) on military service took charge of affairs, had a very anxious talk on the matter in the autumn of 1914. Luckily for them they took Fred into their counsel, and he suggested a solution which under his supervision got them out of difficulties that threatened the Hunt with very great danger—(applause). In concluding, his lordship said he was therefore doubly glad that so many members of the Hunt, both residents and visitors, men and women of all classes, had shown in substantial fashion their appreciation of Fred Goss. It gave him the utmost pleasure to hand him that token of their regard and to offer him with it their grateful thanks for what he had done for the Hunt in the past and their very best wishes for his happiness and prosperity in the future—(loud applause).

ACKNOWLEDGING THE GIFT

First giving Goss a hearty handshake, his lordship, with further words of congratulation, handed to him the cheque. The popular ex-harbourer's reply, though brief, fittingly expressed his appreciation. He thanked them all, he said, from the bottom of his heart for their handsome present and Lord Fortescue for the very kind remarks he had made concerning him. Coming from such an authority on the sport and the particular branch of it with which he (Goss) was associated he valued his lordship's remarks all the more—(applause). He also thanked Mr. Le Bas and the collectors for all the trouble they had taken—(renewed applause).

Hounds immediately moved off, Goss having to wait a little time in order to acknowledge further greetings by friends. A large proportion of the footpeople took up a position above the Punchbowl and at other points in the hope of seeing the hunt develop, but they were doomed to disappointment. Some who had come by car had better luck. Just about two o'clock, Captain Mildmay's second horseman announced that the tufters had found a deer and that the chase was proceeding down the Exe Valley. To cross the hill to Dulverton town and thence up the line of the Exe was an easy run, and before reaching Bridgtown those " on wheels " came up with the hunt. Up to that point there was no deer in front of hounds, but while a string of cars waited in the roadway and many of the field were stationed nearby a fine stag broke covert in full view. What transpired before the *morte* was sounded on the banks of the Haddeo will be gathered from " 'Ware Heel's ! " description of the run, but a good many car people were up in good time to witness the closing scenes between Bury and Harford Mill.

The organisation of the testimonial fund, to which subscriptions were limited to £1, was kindly undertaken by Mr. R. V. Le Bas, of Winsford. In due course a book containing the names of the subscribers will be presented to Goss, but as the lists are not yet closed some time must elapse before the roll is completed.

MEMORIES OF A STAG HARBOURER

FRED GOSS'S THANKS

LADIES AND GENTLEMEN,—As it is impossible for me to thank personally all the subscribers who so kindly contributed to my testimonial that was given to me on Winsford Hill on Saturday last, I would like, through the medium of the *Free Press*, to tender my best thanks to all who contributed, and also to the collectors for their kindness in collecting for the testimonial.

I remain, yours faithfully,

FRED GOSS.

Weir, Dulverton.

INDEX

A

Acland, Sir Francis, 202
Acland, Sir Thomas, 202
Acland, Sir T. D., 136
Acland, Sir Thomas Dyke, 199
Adkins, Major, 116, 119, 130
Allan, Mr. A., 208
Allers Wood, 125, 131
Allotments, 86, 116
Amory, Col. H. H., 107, 108
Amory, Sir Ian, 107–108, 118
Amory, Sir John, 107
Amory, Mr. Ludovic, 165
Anstey Burrows, 114
Anstey Common, stags harboured on, 114
Antlers, 77
— growth of, 79
— history in, 90
— shedding of, 77
— variations in, 84

B

Babbage, J., former huntsman, 178
Badco, Mr., 37, 205
Badgers, habits of, 129
Badgworthy, 51, 94
Bampton, 20
Bampton Fair, 192
Barle, Valley of the, 66, 208
Barle River, 49
Baron's Down, 90, 173, 200

Barton Wood, harbouring in, 71
Basset, Mr. C. H., 25, 93, 201
Bayford, Lord, 28, 51, 54, 60, 63, 86, 94, 130
Bayford Lodge, 90
Bawden, Ernest, present huntsman, 65, 179
Bawden, Mr. J., 65–66
Bellew, Mr. Froude, 96
Berry Hill Wood, harbouring in, 89
Birmingham, Mr. Christopher, 203
Bisset, Mr. Fenwick, 200
Bittiscombe Woods, 95
Blackmore, Jim, 5, 25, 27
Boys Path, 120, 158
Bray Valley, 55, 149
Brendon Two Gates, meets at, 71, 111
Brewer's Castle, 49
Brushford, 65
Burrow Wood, 116
Bury Castle, 129
Buscombe, 98

C

Capel, Mr., 95
Castle Hill, 90, 195, 200
Chains, the, 180
Chains Hoar Oak, 94
Chichester, Sir Arthur, 176
Chorley, Mr., 179

INDEX

INDEX

H

Haddeo River, 20, 95, 105
Haddeo, Valley of, 19, 175
Haddon, 95, 156, 164, 175
Haddon, foxes on, 96
Haddon, hares on, 105
Haddon, meets at, 23, 63
Haddon, winter on, 20
Halberton, 168
Hancock, Mr. Froude, 50, 56, 205
Hantons, 94
Hartford, 19, 103, 167, 175
Hawkcombe Head, 111, 156
Hawkridge, 65, 66, 150, 164
Hawkridge, hunting families of, 66
Hawkridge, meets at, 67, 114
Heal, Arthur, former huntsman, 178
Heathpoult, 159
Hele Bridge, 169, 199
Hele Manor, 107
Henson, Mr., 105
Herbert, The Hon. Col. Aubrey, 123, 167, 209
Herbert, The Hon. Mrs. Aubrey, 209
Higher Combe, 200
Higher Ley Wood, 75
Hill, Mr. A. B., 192
Hind hunting, 91
Hollam Wood, 117
Holm Bush Gate, 202
Holnicote, 90
Hopcott Brake, 58–59
Hornby, Col., 26–28, 162, 201
Horner Farm, 157
Horner Woods, 139, 212
Horner Valley, 130
Hunstone Wood, 69
Hurlstone Point, 24
Hurscombe Wood, 24
Huxtable, Anthony, 24, 178

I

Iron Mill Valley, 193

J

Jodhpur, Maharaja of, 169

K

Kennels, at Hele Bridge, 199
— at Exford, 205
Kestrels, habits of, 125
King's Brompton, 19, 65, 209
Knight, Mr. John, 180
Knight, Sir Frederick, 180

L

Lang, E. J., the present harbourer, 107
Lang, Mr. John, 171
Lang, Mr. Walter, 171
Larkbarrow, 112
Las Casas, Mr. Albert, 93
Le Bas, Mr. R. V., 192
Leeworthy Bridge, 89
Limers, 16
Little, W., 189
Lucas, Mr. Stucley, 200
Luckham, 157
Luxborough, 65, 184
Lydcot Farm, 71
Lydcot Hall, 149
Lydeard, St. Laurence, 187
Lyncombe Farm, 104
Lynton, 68

M

MacDermot, Mr. E. T., 15, 66, 171

INDEX

223

INDEX